We Speak for Peace

To Elizabeth

Ruth Harriet Jacobs

(254)

We Speak for Peace

Ruth Harriet Jacobs, Ph.D.
Editor

KNOWLEDGE, IDEAS & TRENDS, INC.
THE POSITIVE PUBLISHER

First published in 1993 by:
Knowledge, Ideas & Trends, Inc.
1131-0 Tolland Turnpike, Suite 175
Manchester, CT 06040
1-800-826-0529

ISBN 1-879198-08-8
6 x 9 Paper $14.00

10 9 8 7 6 5 4 3 2 1

First Edition
Printed in the United States of America

Cover illustration and design: Gil Fahey
Page design and typesetting: Cindy Parker

Table of Contents

Introduction: A Letter to the Reader

Dear Reader,

You are courageous and realistic to select this book. Most Americans have defended against, run from, and been diverted from recognizing the horror of modern war. They hardly noticed we killed or wounded at least 200,000 humans in the Persian Gulf. Despite the threat of more wars, seeking peace seems so complex, people have turned to smaller, more manageable issues or have privatized their minds and lives.

Subliminal terror and simplification of issues makes people regress to childish states. Feeling disillusioned and impotent in the face of world crises, they become self-obsessed and other-influenced. Made anxious and insecure in a violent world, people blame parents and childhoods for their unhappy lives and the state of the world. They target the family, idolize charismatic leaders and blame givers, join self help groups, see therapists, seek self-improvement, drug themselves, consume media that is violent and pornographic, become hedonistic and selfish, ignore the needy.

This book was created to raise and change consciousness because apathy, escapism, scapegoating, and the need to forget happen after each war.

Between the wars,
they mourn the dead
and hide the wounded
meanwhile arming.

Born in 1924, I have lived through five official American wars and many others supported by my country's armaments and finances. I had a front seat on World War II as a newspaper reporter and later as a volunteer with paraplegic and mentally scarred veterans at the United States Veterans Hospital in West Roxbury, Massachusetts. When I got a B.S. at age 40 at Boston University and a Ph.D. in Sociology at 45 at Brandeis University, I studied war and peace issues and then created a sociology of war and peace course at Boston University and published my research. Of course, people older than I have experienced even more wars and, many, much more directly, such as the war veterans who contributed to this book and the contributors who lost loved ones.

Like many others, in 1991, I was enraged by the killing in the Persian Gulf and by the inability of our own political leaders and other world political leaders to find a peaceful solution. I, with others, took the usual actions available to citizens: phoning, writing to and calling on politicians, picketing, praying, standing in silent vigils. I also decided to collect the words of people who fear and hate war and love and work for peace. Collective words have power—peacepower. We need to counter warpower with peacepower.

I took two tiny ads in two magazines, *Poets and Writers* and *Poet*. The ads requested anti-war pro-peace contributions for an anthology and a short biography, with a deadline of October 1, 1991.

As soon as the magazines were published, poems and prose flooded me both in volume and with tears for their intensity. My standard size R.F.D. outdoor mailbox was filled tight for four months during that summer and fall. Some days, there were so many envelopes that they would not fit in the box; the kind mailperson walked to my house and handed them to me or left them on the porch. I discovered that the ads had been copied in other publications and newsletters such as the International Women's Writing Guild. I had expected hundreds of contributions; I got almost 3,000. Most of the contributors sent multiple pieces, as many as twenty items each. There were very few skinny envelopes.

Writing arrived from people of all ages, people of all 50 United States, people of all occupations. You will see this when you read, as I urge you to do, the brief biographies of the writers. For example, one day's mail was from a parochial school girl, a judge, a Vietnam veteran, a World

War II veteran, a soldier serving in Saudi Arabia, a military officer's wife who asked that she not be identified as such because of military sanctions, an 84 year old man, a machinist, a retired mailman, a physician, a physicist, a nun, a college student, and many others.

Huge boxes filled my house. Many of them had contributions countering what appeared to be the yellow ribbon mania of the time. My mailperson's back began to concern me. When I told friends about the quantity, it was hard for them to visualize this. So one night, I threw out *my* back carrying a huge boxfull to my poetry writing group. The other poets were overwhelmed by the quality, sincerity, and geographical diversity as they pulled envelopes out randomly.

Next I had to find a publisher. I knew I might ask one of the Peace organizations like the War Resisters' League or the Fellowship of Reconciliation or the Women's International League for Peace and Freedom to publish them or perhaps a religious press such as a Quaker Press. I am a Quaker, a member of the Society of Friends, and we are against war and violence. However, I wanted a mainstream press to reach beyond the convinced to the wider public, to you. I knew it would have to be a small press because now, for large publishers, the bottom line is profit. The book might not be profitable. War "adventure" books are profitable, not pro-peace books and anti-war books.

I never dreamed (though secretly prayed) that KIT Press of Manchester, Connecticut, would take on the project. KIT is a rather new press making its way in a difficult market and in hard times. I loved this press which had published my 1991 book, Be an Outrageous Older Woman: A R.A.S.P. Remarkable Aging Smart Person. I discussed the anthology with Sandra Brown, President, and Rita McCullough, Vice President. To my joy, these socially conscious women decided to make a contribution to world peace and take a financial risk to publish this book. I salute their courage.

But the hardest part was ahead. I had to cull to a

few hundred from the thousands of wonderful contributions received. I am a professor who can never fail a student or hardly ever give a C. It was agony to turn down some fine writing and thinking because of lack of space, the need for diversity, and the desire to make as many non repetitive points as possible. I urged the writers in the longest rejection slip on record to send them elsewhere. Perhaps local papers or organizational newsletters or journals or other anthologies will use them or writers will send them out as Christmas or greeting cards. I thank all the writers for their efforts. Many of the rejectees are supporting this book by buying it and telling their networks about it. If it comforts rejectees, I eliminated my own poems to save space.

I hope this book will help Americans to stop escaping and defending against the painful possibility, even probability, of more war. I hope people will be moved to anti-war, pro-peace social and political actions. I thank readers for being willing to experience the emotions of reading this book and for the actions your emotions may inspire. KIT and I would be glad to hear from readers and pass on comments to the individual writers.

On a personal note, for their encouragement, I would like to thank my descendants, Edith Jane Jacobs and Eliha Jacobe, my friends, my colleagues at Regis College and the Wellesley College Center for Research on Women, the Wayland Poets, and members of the Wellesley, Massachusetts Friends Meeting. I especially thank Rita McCullough for her editing and advice and Sandra Brown for her support for this book.

Think and work for Peacepower.

Ruth Harriet Jacobs, Ph.D.
75 High Ledge Avenue
Wellesley, Massachusetts
Retired Sociology Chairperson
Clark University

I

Recruiting, Training, Indoctrinating And Leaving For War

VIDEO GAMES

(written during the bombing of Baghdad by Allied Forces,
January 16-February 26, 1991)

They grew up blitzing electronic enemies
with PacMan and Star Wars.
All it took were quarters, practice,
and the patience to play for hours.

Today, these same boys climb into cockpits,
aim bombs between crosshairs,
and buildings explode
in a puff of smoke.

So high and free,
they smile and cheer,
then zoom away fast.

They do not see
                    the smashed faces
                    bodies burnt to bone.

Removed from the blood
war to them
is like a clean kill video game.

*Carolyn J. Fairweather Hughes, a former communications
specialist, news reporter and editor, now lives in Pittsburgh with
her husband and two daughters.*

ULYSSES

At the Air Show a new surge
of patriotism. Weapons
from the Mid-East war.
Planes, Hum V's and a tank
named Ulysses with the painted
silhouette of two tanks killed.
Stealth Bombers and Patriot
Missles. A stiff-necked crowd
admiring each sleek line,
and hard talk and proud
coming from the old men and boys
about how we'll kick hell
out of anyone who gets in our way.

And under the stars on flags
we hear a rumbling in the tank treads
that go round and round
like figures on an old Greek urn.

Patrick B. Mikulec, born in Honolulu, Hawaii and now living with his wife and son in Aloha, Oregon, teaches high school English.

Recruiting, Training, Indoctrinating,
and Leaving for War

THE GREAT ESCAPE

The recruiters for the army/navy/air force
sit behind plain wooden tables
covered with leaflets on the service,
an officer pictured, bright-eyed and clean,
all his brass buttons shining.

The recruiters, white and clean-shaven,
their close-cropped light hair,
their eyes blue as marbles, stand out in this lobby
at Passaic County College in Paterson, New Jersey
filled with young black/brown skin and voices in ghetto
slang, laughing,
and Puerto Rican women in elastic, day-glo pants,
and slender Latino men with clipped moustaches,
and dapper smiles. Out of the crowd of moving,
circulating students, first Juan Garcia, then Kevin Clark,
drifts over to the recruiters.

I hear the sales pitch on how the service gives you a chance
to learn a trade and to have a career and when you get out,
they even give you a scholarship to college.
Kevin's face turns hopeful, the path
to a better life opening in his mind like a highway
out of this city and the only life he's known,
and Juan listens and he, too, believes.

They drift back to the group. Others replace them.
All day the recruiters talk and talk till finally
at nightfall José Jemenez and Khemi Freeman and George
McKay
and Keisha Lynette return
to the tables, sign their names to long, complicated forms
that they don't comprehend, the path out of the city
smooth as greased metal.

After Broadway,
after the Alexander Hamilton Welfare Hotel,
after the graffiti on the walls,
after the pimp strutting his four women,
after the garbage in the gutters,
after the screaming woman,
this offer, the brass buttons
on the suit of the army lieutenant,
his polished shoes, and the Air Force
corporal, sharp in her blue uniform and neat,
shining hair, seem to hold out golden keys
to José Jemenez, Khemi Freeman, George McKay, Keisha
Lynette
that they hope will set them free.

On T.V. ten days after the outbreak
of the war, the cameraman
takes a picture of some young people
waiting in Saudi Arabia for the fighting
to begin. The camera scans
the untried, untouched faces of the soldiers.
"We've been waiting so long,"
Mason Brown says, "I just want it
to start," meaning the fighting,
the tanks massing at the border,
the ground troops waiting.
"This is where I want to be," he says.

*Maria Mazziotti Gillan has published several books of poetry.
She is the Director of the Poetry Center at Passaic County Community College in New Jersey.*

SEMPER FIDELIS

(Parris Island, SC)

When reveille rushed the surrender of adolescent
dreams, kicked up a chorus of curse and complaint,
we spilled from our bunks, showered half asleep,
razored our stubble, leaped into motley fatigues.

We double-timed to rhythms of "lef—right—
lef—," to stanzas of scatalogical rhymes,
In such an asylum of drab, uniform madness,
even our minds were drilled to soldier along.

What growled at our green platoon seemed hardly human.
Mongrel-eyed, gap-toothed and mastiff-necked,
only the beer-wine-belly dared betray him.
This was Sergeant Bullock, pride of the Corps,

bootcamp spokesman of rank for the martial ideal:
"Not cher guns, you fathead mothers . . ., your WEAPONS!"
Psychopathic mentor to timid recruits,
he delighted in lessons on mayhem, on killing quick.

In the light of close inspection, a confederate moon,
thirsting, hungering (though sucking it in), we whelps,
dragging our tails, fell out on such commands as
"Kill—kill till the bugle calls you home!"

Gus Pelletier is a Professor of English at the State College in Delhi, New York. He is the father of nine children.

SWEAT

"Keep it moving," the booming voice orders
the just-arrived recruits. The buzzing
razor shaves their heads. They must shower,
put on uniforms. They do not yet know
how to lace their boots. For 36 hours,
no sleep. They must run, they must run.
Half moons darken their mottled shirts.
Sweat glistens their faces. They become
one shining mass of youth pressing
towards the distant desert.

The president runs along the beach
in jacket and stocking-cap. Sometimes
he wears a leather hat with peak,
sheep-skin earflaps and the chin strap
left undone. Reporters chase him, extending
microphones. You hear static, the plash of sea,
panting and several rounds of,
"Mr. President, what's new in the war?"
He slows his pace, showing his hardy face
pearled with his efforts. He mumbles,
"I will have a statement later."
Then we hear the chuff-chuff
of his sneakered feet as he presses forward on our native
shore.

Rochelle Natt lives in Great Neck, New York. She is a professional psychic.

Recruiting, Training, Indoctrinating,
and Leaving for War

TEARS AT THE PIER BLUES

My daughter's brown face,
Stares sadly as I leave
I say my daughter's lovely face
Stares sadly as I leave
She waves bye to papa
While our ship moves out to sea.

My wife's smile seems about to crack,
I say my honey's smile is about to crack
Baby jus' pray real hard
For God to bring me back.

I hold back the tears,
This big ole empty world
Says I hold back my tears
In this big ole empty world
Can't bear to leave my wife
And my precious baby girl.

*Twenty-five year old Willie Abraham Howard, Jr. served for four
years as Hospital Corpsman with the United States Navy. He is
a Nursing Assistant, now, in Atlanta, Georgia.*

We Speak for Peace

THIS WAR

Bitterly—she cries;
Listlessly—he goes.
This could have been avoided—
That's what each one knows.

Desperately—he fights . . .
Must she always yearn?
Hopelessly they look on life—
Men will never learn.

+ + +

The average citizen can be
brain washed or emotionally
conditioned to go to war—
whether the war is justified
or not. It is up to those who
can think; who know the
difference between truth and
propaganda, right and wrong;
who will not state their country right when wrong,—and
will not be swayed;—to help
keep us out of wars, thereby
benefiting all.

Artist, poet, song writer and former Coordinator of the Westwood Center for the Arts, Francesca Contessa lives in Westwood, California.

Recruiting, Training, Indoctrinating,
and Leaving for War

II

Anti-War Demonstrations and other Activism

"EXTEND HANDS, NOT ARMS"

said the little banner
        held aloft
            by our rag-tag band:
five old ladies in tennis shoes
        four men in business suits
                three vietvets
        two fringe lunatics
            one mover and shaker
one babe in arms
            and me

but it was too much for them!
        two men shook their fists
            and drove into each other!
        a student on a bicycle read it
            and rammed a hydrant!
a couple stopped to stare
        then agitated in three languages
                with gestures!
            the mayor read it and tried
                not to notice!
        and a bird I thought dead
                quivered in the gutter
        turned over   flapped hard
                and flew

Sheila Golburg Johnson, former high school teacher, writes poems, articles, short stories, and novels in Santa Barbara, California.

PEACE MARCHERS AT THE VIETNAM MEMORIAL

Who would have thought on that cold December in 1969
    when we met, my boots & I, that we'd be here in
    Washington, on my birthday, marching against still
    another war?
We did not think then we would stand here, older now,
    more worn, creased, grey showing at the fray,
among other peace marchers who leave their signs on the
    lawn to stand before this litany of stone,
58,000 points of light etched into the blackness and
    now gone out, not even a flicker,
unless you count those here now, those who remember,
    who tell their children,
Vietnam, Cambodia, Kent State, Jackson State,
who hug each other, who cry, who lean against the wall,
    find names we have not forgotten, some never even
    known, in the worn sole of memory.

When we low-crawled through that night assault exercise
    we did not imagine this pilgrimage along the dusty
    stones of the Mall
in still another grim age like when those on the Wall
    died:
It just goes on & on, from a jungle of politics to a
    desert of values
Kuwait, Tel Aviv, Baghdad, Khafji.

Who would have thought when I applied those acres of
    black polish I would be here to say "no" again—
like that birthday when I sat in the latrine and cried
    for loneliness I don't want to have to do this, I
    want to go home & celebrate my birthday

We came here to wage war on war,
Vermont, Albany, Boston, Toledo,
to the Wall, to weep, to stare, to murmur, hushed as if
        the dead were here,
as indeed they are, in us, in this great crowd that
        even all of them could be lost in.

Who would have thought, who would have thought—at
        least we, my boots and I, can still march,
and when they're gone, I'll buy new boots and boots for
        my children, and keep on marching.

*Dan Wilcox is a member of Veterans for Peace. He now runs a
small press in Albany, New York.*

We Speak for Peace

LITTLE LADY WARRIOR . . .

she stood no
   more than
   four foot four . . .
the little lady warrior
   whose heart
   pumped courage . . .
she linked arms
   with me
in protest against
   the war of '91
   and she sang
words of valor
   in the Chicago night—

an audacious defiance
   glowing in her
   unblinking eyes
Mike Ditka's grabowski
   came to mind . . .
   and I'd willingly
bet this
   little lady warrior
was from a
   working class home . . .
   the resolution defining
facial lineaments
   was pointed—focused
   not a face of
insurrection . . .

"the people united
    will never be defeated . . ."
she sang as we
    advanced step
by protesting step . . .
arms linked
    and our spirits
welded by the
    emotion of the moment . . .
the police mounted
    on horses held
    ebony hued clubs
of our submission
    as they waited
    in anticipation . . .
anxious but resolute.

step by step
    the crowd
    slowly advanced . . .

the chilled night
    air was ablaze
    with conflict as
ideology collided
    with duty . . .
step by step
    the dissenting throng
    approached the waiting
of blue clad
    and duty bound
    officers . . .

the air was tense . . .
a pantomime
    of conflict in the
    neon shadows of
the corporate world . . .
    a flock of pigeons
    huddled under the
bridge . . .
    clouds covered the moon.
the wind was still . . .
    would this be a replay
    of decades past?
a police riot—
    the horses pranced nervously
    their breath wisps of steam
    their eyes widened and wild
    the air was tense . . .

our demonstration
    "the beast for peace"
    had become nearly
demon-like as we
    devoured the moment
    with our
solitary
    sense of mission
    in the
big city night.

the parameters
    of our protest
    had exploded
as we slowly advanced . . .
    the waiting
    line of police
sat erect . . .
    like a line
of vertical
    resistance to the
world's demand
    for peace . . .

Anti-War Demonstrations and
Other Activism

the line wavered
    ever so little . . .
    imaginary bugles
    blared . . .
    the horses snorted . . .
the line of protesters
    advanced . . .
singing for peace . . .
the line of
    police wavered again
    then like the
still waters before a canoe's bow
    they parted to
let us through . . .

she couldn't have
    stood no more
    than four foot four
and yet her
    courage surely dwarfed
    the Standard Oil Building . . .
her onslought of outrage
    her need for peace
    flowed from her
body through our
    linked arms
    and together as one
    the line of
humanity for peace
    advanced . . .

we took the streets
    and laughed . . .
    the beast for peace
had grown claws . . .
    the scream became
    a roar of defiance . . .

our eyes met
    for a brief second
    and we knew
a flash of victory . . .
a moment of our
    time was shared . . .
the atmosphere
    was alive for
    the little lady warrior
and this protesting redskin . . .

*E. Donald Two-Rivers is a full-blooded Indian of the Ojibwa Tribe,
an activist for Equal Rights, a writer, and has appeared on
National Television.*

THE DOUBLE

Father said he was watching the news
& saw someone at the anti-nuclear demonstration
who looked a lot like me. He
had my nose, same color hair,
& was wearing my coat. But he knew
it couldn't have been me, because
this guy was waving at the television camera,
flashing the peace sign, embarrassing
his poor mother & father, & not showing
too much smarts. For why make it easy for those FBI
agents to identify you.
They get good pay, so let them
do a little work by covering your face,
& wearing someone else's coat.

*Hal Sirowitz helped organize demonstrations against the Gulf
War and Committee for Student Mobilization. He is a Special
Education teacher in Queens, New York.*

CIRCLE

Two dozen or so of us
stood in a protest circle
outside the Park Street Station.

We huddled together,
partly to keep warm.
Why don't they ever say

how embarrassing it feels
to have to stand there?
Not thrilling. Not
"nothing better to do."

Some guys came by
with a flag, walked
in a counter-circle around us.
"God Bless America!"
and they shook their fists.

From an office window
a man looked down at us,
held up a hand-lettered sign.
GO HOME it said.

But we *are* home.

Susan Donnelly is a writer, a lobbyist, and an Adminstrator at Harvard University.

PEACE WALK, 1987

A whisper
of beating wings
and whirling winds
over the desert
they came

singing a psalm of peace

Their tears
and the rain
moistened the land
and the earth moved

ever so slightly

In a driving storm's
swirling mist
their chorus surged
sounding their paean
over vast, churning waves

of the sea

With drumming thunder
and flaring lightning
reverberating
throughout the world
they unfurled

banners of protest

Though the missile launched
darkened the dawn
piercing the skies
and pilgrims
weeping

We Speak for Peace

at the gates

the sun breaking through
warmed
the drenched earth
trembling with
seeds of

Shalom.

Joanne Herrmann, former teacher, Pax Christi member, and head of the Nuclear Freeze Coalition in Clearwater, Florida, now lives with her husband and three children in Jacksonville.

FOR THE
WAR ON WAR

We rode buses from rural-tune places;
from cities of music, chiming with love
for the planet our medley embraces.

Our emotions were winging an outstretching dove,
sailing dreams and sharp prayers that would splinter
mankind from such frights as hawk flights, with our shove.

"DEMAND A NUCLEAR FREEZE," the printer
had frosted on placards we carried,
"OR ACCEPT A NUCLEAR WINTER!"

And it seemed every dissident-rebel had married
on Washington's Mall, to merge into one voice
that pleaded and wailed and harried . . .

The Bill of Rights grants us a wide range of choice,
but its authors were lacking one qualm
we'd provoke in our time for new cause to rejoice,

because virtue to bless every grandchild with calm
sleeps in this amendment— "FREEDOM FROM THE
BOMB."

*John Balkwill is a freelance writer living in Hampton,
Virginia.*

1/16/91

Our man of the hour, our man of power, stays dis-
creetly out of sight, but lets it be known he has peace in his
heart. Behind the curtains of his house, he chooses to
ignore the street people with their words of protest pinned
to their clothing, he chooses to ignore the belated pleas for
peace that come for all reasons, from many places. And he
smiles, because now he *is* a man of power, because it is his
decision, because it is to him that the pleas come. The
other men, mostly white like him, like his house of power,
those who have spent their lives arranging to be with him at
this hour, exchange firm handshakes. They all feel the
quiet, full machismo of what they wield, over the lives not
their own. Grim, but powerful; it is peaceful between them,
they know they are making history, they know that control
is better remembered than correctness, that waging war
commands greater attention than haggling over peace.
They are more interested in being the men of the hour than
men of honor. Our man of power says to the world that he
has peace in his heart, he takes a deep breath, and he
sighs, and he signs, and there is war.

*Ellie B. Belen has been a bus driver, a truck driver, a produce
broker, a bookkeeper, a printing press operator, and a
groundskeeper. Now, she is a writer.*

Anti-War Demonstrations and
Other Activism

She Wrote to Stop Aid to El Salvador

SHE WROTE TO STOP AID TO EL SALVADOR
SHE WROTE TO PREVENT THE WAR SHE WRO
TE TO PROTEST THE CONTRAS IN NICARAG
UA SHE WROTE TO STAY OUT OF GRENADA;
SHE TRAVELED TO WASHINGTON SHE TRAV
ELLED TO NEW YORK CITY TO KEEP THE U
S OUT OF THE MIDDLE EAST SHE KEPT VI
GILS AT RECRUTING STATIONS AND CONG
RESSMAN MRAZEK'S OFFICE IN 90° AND 3
0° TO PREVENT THE DEATH OF 250,000 I
RAQI MEN WOMEN AND CHILDREN..AND THE
BOTTOM LINE: IT ALL CAME TO NOTHING!

*Joan Payne Kincaid was once a concert-opera singer. She now
paints and writes in SeaCliff, New York.*

THE DESERT STORM STAMP

The old woman was handed a row
of round gold medals, bright
as coins hanging from precise
military stripes, the ribbons
crisp colorful columns
of red, blue and black.
She paid and backed off
from the long post office line
reading the small print:
Honor Those Who Served . . .

Holding the stamps
at attention she wished she'd
been given birds, trees, flowers.
They were wonderful young men
and women, like the kids next door
but she was opposed
to this business of war.
To advertise, approve, glorify it
ran against her peace-loving grain.
Surely the earth was the victim
and everyone lost something
precious in this oil-fueled war.

But the stamps were a trifle.
Should she resist? Return them?
Make a fuss over such clean dignified
corners, the innocent pale sky
holding the emblems of honor?
It seemed foolish to destroy them,
so she licked and pasted the stamps
on her letters. Placed a ? mark
by each one. Yes, she thought,

Question war. Question war.

Bernice Rendrick has worked for an insurance company, a retail store, and a hospital. She is now past her 60th birthday and too busy to figure out how to slow down.

Anti-War Demonstrations and
Other Activism

III

War: A Review & Record

READINESS

Grinding	the stone ax
chipping	the flint knife,
forging	the throwing spear,
balancing	the javelin,
stretching	the bowstring,
sharpening	the saber,
locking	the bayonet into place,
priming	the cannon's vent
cocking	the flintlock,
pulling	the pin on a hand grenade,
aligning	the mortar's trajectory,
loading	the magazine of a submachine gun,
yielding	the howitzer's firing lanyard,
feeding	the round to an automatic rifle,
sighting	the rocket launcher
elevating	the heavy machine gun,
thumbing	the cartridge into a rifle's firing chamber,
inserting	the magazine into the base of a pistol
maneuvering	the tank for a blitzkrieg,
launching	the combat aircraft,
targeting	from a long-range radar system,

we are ready since dawn,
weapons glaring
over all things
from fresh snow to field mice,
waiting against this day
for the pale hand of someone else
to target us all,
to draw back a missile in a metallic bowstring
and blow moon and sun to bits.

R. Nikolas Macioci teaches in a high school and wins prizes and awards for his poetry in Columbus, Ohio.

THE PRICE

The Revolution, 4,435,
War of 1812, 2,260,
Civil War, 364,511
(not counting those who died
under the Stars and Bars),
Spanish American War, 2,446,
World War I, 116,516,
World War II, 405,339,
Korea, 54,246,
Vietnam, 58,135,
and still counting.
Nine-hundred and eight thousand
Six-hundred twenty-one.
That, brothers and sisters
And children yet unborn,
Is the sum.
For the red, the white, the blue,
For "We the people . . ."
A heavy price due.

R.A. Horne founded Free Speech Foundation, Inc., to work to
secure our First Amendment rights. He has been a victim of
political oppression.

CRADLE TO GRAVE: Notes on an Excavation

In the deepest layer, settlements are simple,
ample homes of equal size. The few goods—
clay cradles, tools, carved toys—
lack evidence of ownership or tribute.

Royal quarters dominate the next layer,
ringed by smaller dwellings. We uncover gold
jewelry and a crudely embellished shield.
An elaborate code in clay, genesis of all writing,
compels repayment and exacts taxes.
Upon tombs, the deceased in bas-relief
each bear some individual likeness: baldness,
a mass of curls, a less-upturned archaic smile
beneath a warrior's helmet.

In the most recent layer, weaponry grows
more elaborate and richly decorated
while all civilian ornament vanishes. Gold
is stacked as bricks. Grave sculpture,
too, has disappeared, as if identification
were deeply feared. This impulse for security
spurs a regression in design:
depressed bedchambers without windows,
armored cages for doors.
The vaulted architecture at this late stage
so favors subterranean rooms
we can no longer distinguish their homes
from their tombs.

*Lee Patton is a member of Amnesty International, the
Denver Center Playwrights Workshop, Colorado Dramatists, and
the Leaping Berylians. He is a teacher.*

PATRIOTISM

World War I,

George M. Cohan's "Over There,"
"The War to end all wars."

World War II,

Rationing, sugar, gasoline, butter, coffee, . . .
Betty Grable's war bond rallies,
Kate Smith's "God Bless America,"
"Rosie, the Riveter," women in the work force.

Korean War,

Flag draped caskets, "Taps,"
Veteran's parades.
Loved ones waited
for the eleven o'clock news,
and the names of the dead.

Vietnam War,

A monument trying to make amends.

Nancy Levins is fifty-eight, a mother of two, grandmother of five, and a devoted wife. She received a degree in Arts this year.

FROM BIRTH TO ADOLESCENCE:
AS AN ADULT: LEARNING TO SAY THE WORD AGAIN

1957/1958

My oldest sister and myself
were conceived under the sign
of President Dwight D. Eisenhower.
As infants, learning to crawl in this new world
of ours, we were unaware
that Vice President Richard M. Nixon
flew to Asia
to analyze, and to report to Eisenhower
the political unrest in Vietnam.

1959/1960
A baby sister joined my oldest sister and myself;
We ABCed, 123ed, tied our shoes,
and Dr. Suessed our imaginations,
while the Vietnam confrontation continued.
Vietnam had three syllables;
Kukla, Fran, and Ollie never used that word
when they entered our living room,
and taught us about childhood friendships.
They talked about China, not Vietnam.

1961
Another sister joined the three of us,
while an elected Savior, President John F. Kennedy,
established the Peace Corps
to help underdeveloped countries.
With Vietnam, he sent military advisors.

1962
The advisors President John F. Kennedy
sent to Vietnam did not end the war;
more advisors were needed, along with military aid.

1963

Military men were shipped overseas.
Fighting happened in jungles, and swamps,
but racial tension created unrest at home.
While in Texas, President John F. Kennedy,
filmed on a home movie camera, died,
because of an assassin's bullet.
Vice President Lyndon Baines Johnson,
originally from Texas, became the President.
My three sisters and myself questioned,
Will the war stop?

1964

Another son had been born into the family.
With two sons and three daughters, the parents
questioned how long the war would last.
Would it last until our oldest son reached the age of eighteen?
For on the news, President Lyndon Baines Johnson
sent more troops to Vietnam.
On the evening news, soldiers died on the black-and white,
soldiers wounded, Vietnam civilians cried,
villages torched,
an unknown man picked birthdays from a large drum;
the next day the names were printed in the newspaper.
The oldest son checked the newspaper
to find his birthday.
had it been chosen?
Will Dad fight in Vietnam?

1965/1966/1967

The war escalated.
President Lyndon Baines Johnson sent in more troops,
more young men.
The black-and-white nightly news kept track
of the dead Vietnamese, and the dead Americans.
Like a baseball/basketball, or football game,
the scores were recorded.
The five children watched,
wondering who was winning the game.

1968
While the students, including the five children,
learned about prejudice, and war in grade school
President Lyndon B. Johnson decided to reduce
the number of troops sent to Vietnam;
he also decided not to seek political office
for another term.
In the midst of the longest war with the most casualties,
Robert Kennedy and Martin Luther King were assassinated.
Father told his five children that he built
top secret mechanical parts for the war;
a question arose, Could the economy thrive on peace?

1969
Thousands of young people congregated in New York State
for the Woodstock concert, hearing the music of Joan Baez,
Jefferson Airplane, Blood, Sweat and Tears,
Janis Joplin, and Jimi Hendrix;
the concert-goers tried to levitate the Pentagon.
Man planted the first U.S. flag on the moon.
A triumph for Man, and the United States, yet the war
ravaged,
despite President Richard M. Nixon withdrawing troops.
Another son was born into the family,
and the oldest son wondered, Will I have to fight
in Vietnam when I turn eighteen?

1970
The youngest son was born into the family;
the four sons and three daughters heard about drugs.
Janis Joplin, Jimi Hendrix overdosed.
They were spokesmen for the young generation.
Their music inspired others:
students protested throughout the United States:
Berkeley, Columbia, Southern Illinois,
and at Kent State four students were shot
by the National Guard.
A young woman in a black-and-white newspaper photo-
graph

raised her arms slightly in the air,
and cried, cried.
Her immortal pose,
her expression speaking for the nation.
President Richard M. Nixon declared a cease-fire.
Peace talks would begin.

1971
No parades.
No bandwagons.
No celebrations of exaltation.
The troops were home, on U.S. soil.
Vietnam, with only three syllables,
became a word hushed-hushed.
Vietnam,
hundreds of thousands of North/South Vietnamese died,
hundreds of thousands of Americans died.
Vietnam,
year after year, radio, television, newspapers, magazines,
played and replayed the war scenes,
until the nation became immune to the word.
And then silence.
"The Deer Hunter," "Coming Home," "Platoon,"
"Born on the Fourth of July,"
sent an invitation to the nation
to re-experience the fighting in Vietnam,
but more, to understand the vets, and promote peace.
Churchill "V"ed, Nixon "V"ed, the hippies "V"ed:
Victory, Peace.
The nations of the world "V"ed.

A special note: the oldest daughter joined
the Army in 1976.
She served three years.
The youngest son joined the Marine Corps Reserves in
1991.

*Paul A. Hanson is employed as a set-up man in a paper box
plant. He is a descendant of Rebecca Nurse, hanged in Salem,
Massachusetts, 300 years ago.*

PORTRAIT IN RED

Gleaming bayonets were the artists' brushes
And young men's blood the paint.
Munitions makers were the Rembrandts
And fields of green the canvas
Of a portrait to be painted in red.

Death was the art connoisseur,
The wealthy dark lady in waiting,
Who would pay gold for the portrait in red.

The Rembrandts were proud of their masterpiece,
That Satan, himself, had inspired.
Proud of this thing they created,
A portrait of hate by the hated,
Painted with bayonets for brushes
And young men's blood the paint!

-yves h. lacaze worked in almost every phase of censorship in World War II. He has been writing against war and for peace for many years. He is 76 years old.

LOOKING BACK

I. The Eighties

The Israeli soldier wrote that, from his tank,
war was like watching TV. He shot; men fell;
and that was all. He never thought
that it was real.

II. The Seventies

The historian wrote that war had changed,
that the battlefield had become
an empty place. Men died
without ever seeing the enemy.
Men clumped together under cover,
endured hostile fire,
shot back at trees.
It didn't seem real.

III. The Fifties

The men remembered small things:
a woman's hand cupped around steaming tea,
pants that wouldn't stay up,
lice in the hair and dysentery.

IV. The Forties

Photographers tried to remember
everything, to bring it all home,
to edit the images to make them meaningful.
It doesn't seem real.
Black and white, grainy, marching
through newsreels—
memoirs in hardback, letters from friends—
textbooks on strategy—
the picture that matters

is the image of the winding stair,
reaching up into the heavens,
seared onto the wall in Hiroshima
by the star that fell,
who cannot be forgiven.

But the war our kids remember
is the one John Wayne fought
and they saw it for real
in the movies.

Dulce et decorum est
pro patri mori.

*Tina Quinn Durham is a graduate student at Arizona State
University. She is also a desktop publishing specialist. Her
brother and her grandfather were military men.*

THANK YOU

Thank you wall. Thank you air for not ionizing.

It's 6:42 in the Midwest.

Thank you Bush, Reagan, Carter, Ford, Nixon, Johnson, Kennedy, Eisenhower.
  Thank you President Truman for doing it only twice.
Thank you Peacemaker, Pershing, Cruise, Nautilus, Polaris, Titan, MX.
Thank you 200,000 microchips times 200,000 microchips times 200,000 microchips.
  Thank you 47 orders to "Fire!" for being discovered as accidents.
Thank you Three Mile Island. Thank you Chernobyl.
  Thank you, big accident, for not happening.

It's 6:43pm in the Midwest.

Thank you Gorbachev, Chernenko, Andropov, Breshnev, Kosygin, Kruschev, Bulganin, Stalin.
Thank you Batwing, Scud, SSX-24, SS-20, IRBM, ICBM, MIRV.
Thank you older generation. Thank you my generation. Thank you younger generation.
Thank you maniac. Thank you neurotic. Thank you normal person for not ending it all. Thank you two keys for not turning.
Thank you, earthquake, for not cracking SIOP's headquarters, Nebraska.

It's 6:44pm in the Midwest.

Thank you mind for keeping track. Thank you mind for usually keeping the process hidden.
Thank you billions and billions and billions of dollars spent on the last six minutes. Thank you last six minutes for not happening.

Thank you regional conflicts for not going nuclear. Thank
  you Korea, Viet Nam, Cambodia, Nicaragua, Afghani-
  stan, South Africa, Iran, Iraq. Thank you, Saddam
  Hussein, for moving slowly.
Thank you, spontaneous combustion. Thank you air.
  Thank you walls for not vaporizing.

It's 6:45pm in the Midwest.

Thank you USA, USSR, China, England, India, France,
  Sweden, Pakistan, maybe Israel, Argentina, South Af-
  rica.
Thank you. Thank you.

*Clive Matson lives in Oakland, California and makes his living
teaching "Crazy Child" writing workshops. He enjoys masters
sports and collecting minerals in the field.*

WAR THE WORLD OVER

over
there
somewhere
there
is
WAR

over
here
somewhere
there
is
more
WAR

when
there
and
here
are
somewhere
then
somehow
we are
all
supposed
to
be
at
WAR

when WAR
is
everywhere
then
here

and
there
have
no
place
else
to
go
and
when
the
world
loses
it
self
to
WAR

then
there
won't
be
any
where
any
more.

D. Nico Leto is an instructor in the field of rape prevention education and a world political organizer. She co-edited the Italian American Women's issue of SinisterWisdom, *"il viaggio delle donne."*

LET US HATE ONE ANOTHER

Let us sit down together
and hate one another right now.

Fists raised high
swear dedication
'til death do us part;

Repetitiously
send sweet young men
far off to die.

In the media's red glare
smiling old men
congratulate themselves.

Another job well done.

Mothers will still come
searching the names
carved out in death
rained down on black stone.

Claire Michaels is a poet, writer, performing and visual artist. She is a teacher, an actress, and a woman of great courage who has overcome obstacles of overwhelming magnitude in her life.

BLOW UP THE WORLD

(a performance piece)

Women
Men
We all got the urge to start again
Start over   Start again   Start over   Start again
What is it in me wants to blow up the world?
Moral Majority   Daddy's authority
Right To Life and Born Again
My sister   My cousin   Some of my friends
Ronald Reagan is my father
Nancy is my mother's dream
I come from them
I'm the blood of them
I hate myself in them
They hate the selves they see in me
What is it in us wants to blow up the world?
What is it in us wants to blow up the world?

I drink too much   You smoke too much
He eats too much   She sweats too much
Too much too much it's all too much
Lite beer   Lite smokes   Lite Aunt Jemima
God is lite   One calorie   Hallowed be   Thy name
Diet cocaine   Life against death   Crystal meth
Give us head
'Till we're dead
Watch your weight   Learn who to hate
Weight Watcher Pizza   Watch your neighbor eatcha
Watch him on the street   Watch him steal your TV set
Watching watching   The world is watching
The only challenge left is the Pepsi Cola Challenge?
Do you stand on White Rock?   Punk rock?   Hot cock?
or money money money money money money money
MONEY?
What is it in me wants to blow up the world?

Meditate   Cogitate   Agitate   Regurgitate
What is in what's on your plate?
Nihilistic   Anarchistic   Vapid   Void   and Ballistic
First Strike   Lucky Strikes
Three strikes and you're . . .
God's not dead
She's a disabled wife in a welfare line
She's lyin' on the street   She ain't got no feet
God's not dead   He's a Vietnam Vet just doin' his time
He's a junkie alcoholic out of his mind
His hands in the air   He ain't got no hair
They ain't got nowhere to go

Go to jail   Go to jail
Go directly to jail
Get your mail   Get your mail
From the IRS
Sayin' pay up   Or confess
You're life is a mess
Turn your sister in
Turn your parents in
Turn yourself in
Know all the facts   Pay your missile tax
And relax   You've got Master Charge
Go ahead   Charge ahead   Kill 'em dead   Beat your head
Against the wall   Big bank   Big bark
Loan shark   Big stick   Big dick
Big bucks   Big trucks   Life sucks
And then you die
Die-hard   Dye job   Nose job   Blow job
Get a dead-end job
Can't trust   Can't love
Can not relate   Participate
What is it in me wants to blow up this world?

Let them eat bombs   Make more bombs
The bomb is peace   Give us a big piece
Get more crazy   Join the Navy

Take it out on yourself
Take it out on someone else
Dyke   Faggot   Queer
Drink more beer
Can't get it up?
Beat your mother up
Shoot it all up
Blow it all up
Go to war   Go to war
Go directly to war
First strike   Lucky Strikes
Three strikes and you're
out   Take it out   Take it out on yourself
Out take it out   Take it
out on someone else
Nigger   Spick   Prick
Commie   Chink   Wop
Doo wop   Doo wop
Honkey   Junkie   Jew
Scoobie doobie do
Butch   Fairy   Femme
Kill all of them   Kill all of them
What is it in me wants to—
What is it in me wants to blow up—
What is it in me wants to blow up this world?
What is it in you wants to blow up this world?
What is it in them wants to blow up this world?
What is it in us wants to blow up this world?
Blow it Up?

Chocolate Waters, award winner free-lancer, writer, poet, lives and works in New York City.

IMPASSE

I've lived with live ammo long enough!
Time for a little R & R.
I'm shell-shocked, in thrall, locked
And never out of sight of the front line fight.
Any time off for good behavior?
Can medals bullet-proof the heart?
Hey—I'm ready to retreat
All the way back to before this war.
Can't undo what's done?
Just call a truce.
Peace at any price?
How nice!

Carol O'Brien works part-time as a cataloger at a public library, skis part-time with her husband and family, and is a part-time poet who wishes there were more hours in each day.

ON NOT BEING AT THE MISSILE BASE

What have I known of violence or of war,
not cowardly—retreating willfully—but confined
by disposition—yes, class and even race—
it's easy to blame genes. Yet, what blame?
"Dog eat dog" existence, "Live free or die"—
glory in the gut and head, fighting "the good fight."

Darwin and disciples insist the species fight
for dominance. The survivors of that war
develop a stronger wing or pod or else they die.
"It is better to have lived and lost . . ." Confined
by a crooked spine or sightless eyes—not your blame—
you are an obstacle and will oppress the race.

"The weak shall inherit . . ." nothing in this race—
pigeons, redwoods, whales unprepared to fight.
Certain, Tasmanian natives are to blame
for being dead. Uncivilized to schemes of war,
the subtleties of the white man's brain, they were confined
for their "salvation." Who encouraged them to die?

"The proof in living is in knowing how to die"
exonerates; does not exalt the human race.
Whether he accepts, rebels, man is confined
by the span of breath and so defined. The decision to fight
is praised by deific majority—progress. War
against poverty, crime. Attack whatever's to blame.

The peony dwindles, the planet ends—what blame?
Will this inquiry cause anything *not* to die?
As if revealing some tainted fruit prevents a war,
as if sin were a truth. Atalanta won the race
not to relish her suitors' heads. How otherwise fight
the fatal loss; assure the omens stay confined?

If I have not been to Saigon or Salvador, confined
to the slings of lesser outrage, find in respite, blame,
I am as absurd as those who long to fight.
Is protest worthless without the willingness to die?
to sense the obscene death? I see joggers race,
determined mouth and eyes, eluding or lusting after war.

Blame not Tortoise for succeeding in the race.
Nor doom Hare to die for losing in this "fight."
Make war into a fable, or Fool, stay by war confined.

*Marilyn Jurich teaches at Suffolk College in Boston,
Massachusetts, and is legally blind.*

DEATH DOESN'T CARE

mobilize metal
mobilize green
mobilize bodies
war is obscene

travel on tankers
travel by air
travel together
death doesn't care

shoot at your shadow
shoot at the sun
shoot when you're ready
re-load your gun

kill other soldiers
kill when you're told
kill some civilians
pause to re-load

watch all your friends die
watch all the gore
watch all the news shows
do you want more?

time to go home now
time for a break
time for your mother
to cry at your wake

war's on the tv
war's in the air
war's getting hungry
death doesn't care

Barrie Gellis is an English teacher and a TV producer for Public Television who believes compassion will save the world, lubricated with humor.

July 15, 1991

Dear Ms. Jacobs:

This coming October I reach the three-quarter century mark. Not an unusual occurrence as birthdays go, but a personal astonishment. (It is my guess that the vast majority of us are indestructibly young and cannot quite make the connection between chronological time and the beginningness that is heart/mind.)

Having lived a long time, I have seen too much of war, all kinds. I was born during World War I, married and had children during World War II, did what I could to raise them during the Korean "engagement" and Vietnam, and still it goes on. A madness beyond the powers of words to express. We are taught to pay attention to the "outside world". We are not taught to listen to ourselves, nor are we given guidance on how to find our own joy. So, as I see it, importances are put aside unrecognized, and the result is war of one kind or another.

Sincerely,

Loretto M. Kelly

Ms. Kelley's letter is as eloquent a force for peace as her poem is (see next page). Ed.

UNHOLY TRUTH

Very quietly, much too quietly,
or with deafening bombast
if I can't contain myself,
I take things and put them aside.
The quietness as the bombast
is camouflage for the heart of the matter
which doesn't put anything aside
and, to boot, is always looking.
Nothing is put aside but dies of it,
gets ulcers, cries, lies, denies,
collides with dense objects,
or habituates to its own grotesque
within the someday syndrome.
Even goes to bloody war
weeping streams of regret
(much as willow trees willow),
dallying with things which are people,
dreams, the possible, the probable,
and always the highly likely.

Thereafter (and unavoidably should it
go as cleverly far as war),
by the power of the hidden longing
thrusting the unicorned mountain,
and by the radiance of jeweldom
releasing its empire of buried sound,
the put aside rises resurrect of outrage,
and manifests with multiple heads,
maws, jaws, claws, beaks, teeth,
eyes, knives, guns, bombs, gases,
and missiles of fire which burn,
tear, spear, pierce, bite, chew,
grind, and thoroughly eat up.
It is total consumption and no chance
for the good death. The put aside dies
but not untormented. In one evasive way
or another it speaks unholy truth.

PAGANS
(a reading)

There will be a lake so the head must move from side to side. Far away from any war the mists lift over the opposite shore. Volcanoes show themselves dimly through a muslin haze. Turning to see another kind of expanse a woman looks at a man. She will love him today. There will be no hours to pace. He will be afraid to love her. He is here from far away. She will hum "Your Country-Ness." The diaphanous scenery the song urge on his desire to love this woman. Far away wives are moving furniture. Far away children need what they cry for. Far away children with nothing from little feel too weak to cry. When they cry they die in their own sound. Far away they number between sixty-five and eighty percent and they survive unlike the wild salmon the quetzal or so many species. Far away the young are waging war with stones. Somewhere if they reach the stage to over populate they become the violent majority. They begin to be entrepreneurs on the free market selling very dear parts of themselves. If they reach the age of young adults they exist perforated by holes. Close to home the law of the land is a business card. Closing in profits prevent wages for work already spent. Far away through automated hearts larceny worms its way to the surface. Far away the homeless and tulips share the same park. Far away lawyers prepare the defense for a girl raped. Far away a woman boards a train in Soweto. It is dark. It is morning. Far

away   the people sit hunched   eat rice at the edge of a
river. Far away   hidden in the early past   the Black Berets
take a Huk leader. The young men do as they are told.
They rarely tell their top secret story. That's what intoxi-
cants are for   to enforce the forgetting. That everyone
forgets the million plus dead in Vietnam. In Central
America   the years adding up to generations   dying in
wars that don't count. That everyone remembers nutmeg
and Noriega is enough. Far away   the media ignores the
whole story beginning with ancient history. Far away   in
Mesopotamia   smart bombs hone in on targets with ears
eyes   noses   fingers   toes and the heart and brain that
make the total anatomy associate closely pain and hate.
Closing in   starwars ignite the fireworks to celebrate the
claiming of oil   finite   and for sale   for profit only. To
honor bloodletting in the sands. To personalize by remote
control a takeover putting another people into bondage
again and in another way. Far away   a journalist calling
home   submits a story   and it disappears. Far away   in
these hours   in this steel-grey cold   during the slow walk
home. To the undressing   to the bed   to the long measure
of giving.

*Zoe Angelesey teaches poetry to youth at El Centro de la Raza
and writing at Seattle Central Community College. She is editing
a collection of interviews with modern jazz musicians.*

ODE TO AUTUMN — 1940

Autumn, come bless us. Bring the ripening days,
The light spilled on the world as clear as glass,
Contented crickets refilling their full cup
                    as minutes pass.

Now through the kitchen window steals a sense
Of struggle ended, of the steady sun
Caressing and perfecting without haste;
                    Man's labor done.

                    * * *

Autumn, come bless us—we whose children lie
Like hail-threshed crops upon the battle field;
Whose trees of hope, twisted, uprooted, rent,
                    Will give no yield.

We who from city to city,
leaving no stone on a stone,
Fled; who have planted no seed, who call no blade
                    Of grass our own.

Autumn, come bless us. Raise what we did not sow
To be our bread,
Lest we for food turn to our fields accursed,
                    And find our dead.

Elizabeth Lindemann wrote this poem before she reached 30 and was struggling to clarify her thinking about war and non-violence. Now at 79, she is a member of the Society of Friends and a confirmed pacifist.

LATENCY

Chimney stacks
were stalked
with smoke—
caught and curled
hearts vaporized
charred unfurled
rose in vent
marled inside.
A puff of eye
cast out a hole
daubed the sky—
sharp scented
white silt
soft breeze
blew out
bare bones
slubbing screams
whispering moans.

Forty years—Bitberg.
"Chimney Ah well!
Aren't the cumulus
heaped lovely swell?
Careful   Step gently
S S tumulus."
Scraps of cries—
a herd of charred
tongues shriek—
crossed stones
a swath of eyes whirr—
scythed sickle
gasping pains recur—
koshered
cursing koans slur
coursing paths
of flesh.

*D.P. Murphy is a family therapist and an English teacher in
Lowell, Massachusetts. He loves his wife, his three children and
his work.*

A FRIENDLY WORD FROM OUR SPONSOR

RAID: Annoying People Killer
     Formula 5

     Kills Folks Dead!
     Clean, Pleasant Scent

Three cheers for progress!
Now you can kill those
Pesky people and not be
Troubled by the unpleasant
Odor of decomposing humans.

Kids be the first on your
Block to kill your parents with
Toxins ordered from our neato
Advertisements in the back
Pages of your favorite
Comic Books!
Men don't fret;
There's an ad right
Next to the Pet of the Month.
So stock up now
Buy early buy often
While our supply lasts.
Use our handy-dandy coupon
For increased savings!

Just remember,
The more RAID
You own, the less chance
Your enemy will want to
Spray you; so,
Fill up your cellars
With RAID and feel secure
In us.

This has been a paid political announcement.

EPILOGUE: EARTH

Ash snow
Settles on rubble.
Your home.
My home.
No home.

Charred children
Smolder along barricades
Under another
Lightless day.
Emaciated dogs
Pick indiscriminately
Through stale carcasses
Snarling.

Public swimming pools
Mass graveyards
Radiation scarred bodies
Struggle to regain a
Humanity
Forever lost
To the Great God,
Hatred.

Their fault.
Our fault.
God's fault.
Fuck fault.

It seems that Charon
Could not ferry sufficient
Souls across
To satisfy the increasing demand;
So
Brought hell
To earth.

Robert B. Nejman's ambition in life is to become a Muppet, but in the meantime he is a stand-up nihilist. He is working on a master's degree at SUNY, Fredonia, New York.

PEACEMAKER

To be a peacemaker one begins
by renouncing war, the last
resort of solving conflict.

First, there's talk, round and
round, like snakes reaching
for their tails. Negotiate, demand,
concede, disguise the threat in
diplomatic terms, meaning more
than spoken words declare.

When charades and minuets
withdraw, the end unreconciled,
and war's announced
in patriotic oratory, what
does then the peacemaker do?

His conscience governs passion,
principle abhors the bellicose
on either side. Where will he stand?
When means and ends don't reconcile
he's philosophically correct,
but bombs will leave him dead.

*Eighty-five year old Daniel Green is a veteran of World War II.
He was discharged as a major having served in China, Burma,
and India. He has been writing for three years.*

WAR
for Sonia Sanchez

War

    is

        Men

          and Machines

            killing Men

And people

        Men

          Women

            Children

              Dying Dying Dying

War

    is

        Green Teenage Marines

            Decapitated

Headless bodies

        skipping across the sands

Immobile bodyless heads

          mouths opened in terror

Screaming silently

Mamma, Mamma

I don't want to die

Oh why, oh why, oh why

Astoria Red (pen name) is a former New York City taxi driver and a rejected Vietnam volunteer turned war resistor.

WAR GAMES

Do all men possess an innate proclivity
    Toward any war-like activity?
Do they get a surge of adrenaline
    That courses through their veins?
Does it inspire their curiosity
To see people display their animosity
Do they mutually conspire at the prospect of war
    No matter what the pain,
    No matter what the gain?
War movies, war games,
    All projections of the same
Just a dress rehearsal
Someone else to blame
For their own inadequacy.

*Marie-Louise Meyers is a wife for 31 years, mother of three
outstanding children, teacher now beginning a new chapter in
the book of life; she loves to commune with nature.*

THE DREAMERS

Combat is all right if the other men
    are dark or lighter. If the women
        are hairy, this will ease our

burden, such animals they are.
    If they live in huts with no power
        lines, this is another plus.

                    *   *   *

Always bomb the bridges, the walkways
    of persistent memories, linking lives
        and times, under which the moon floats,

starting human dreams. The other
    learning places—in and under trees,
        in sleeping places, at the edges of gardens—

the private sanctuaries of desire or
    fascination; strafe these,
        with our blonde eyes on the spidery

cross hairs of sights with dead centers,
    these places where hamburgers and pizza
        have yet to be invented.

Their brown-eyed, dark-skinned gods
    won't interfere. Our god of light
        stands with a flashing sword

we've forged from gold and given
    others like it to marines, each
        with one foot on a beach somewhere.

We might be afraid they could dream
    us away, the way we left off dreaming,
        because we were afraid

of the worst dream of all,
    that we've stopped living,
        that there's something we've forgotten.

Peter Desy is an Associate Professor at Ohio University in Lancaster, Ohio, where he attempts to raise bonsai trees. Edward Mellen Press will publish a book of his poetry this year.

PUSH BUTTON WORLD

Push button — room is white.
Push button — room is black.

Push button — window opens.
Push button — window closes.

Push button — carrots become juice.
Push button — garbage disappears.

Push button — tank fires gun.
Push button — world goes away.

Mary Rutkorsky-Ruskin has lived in Alaska, Connecticut, Massachusetts, Istanbul, Paris and a small island in Greece. She also practices shiatsu and kyu do-Zen archery.

THUNDER JETS ASSORTED FRUIT FLAVORS SQUADRON

> a children's snack that has the "B-2
> Stealth Bomber, so *top secret* that it's
> not included in every package."

The Pentagon told us that it did not exist,
even though it's been flying since 1981
in the high subsonic range of 600 mph.
Its dark delta wings can slip through borders in the night,
penetrate radar defenses, bomb targets before the enemy
reacts.
Funded by the black budget, in the secret heart of the
bureaucracy
where items are buried in the confluence of sweet talk and
lies,
it now costs more than if it were made of solid gold.
The generals boast about its ebony wings,
the exponential capabilities of its warheads,
the possibility that the final consummation will be
a frenzied nuclear spasm, the ultimate circle jerk . .   . .

*Barbara Crooker divides her time among writing, sharing
interests and activities with her three children, and raising
vegetables, herbs and perennials in Fogelsville, Pennsylvania.*

WAR ZONE

He lived many
nightmarish years,
in a setting
of calculated destruction.
In a war zone inhabited by just a few.

It wasn't until long after
he had escaped,
that he realized those
who led him through
each battle, should have long ago
given up useless fight
and moved into
neutral ground.

Deloris Selinsky holds a degree in Political Science and a Master's in Human Resources Management.

WAITING

We inhabit a strange, loose world
     shifting so rapidly we can't see the pivots.
     I'm shocked! A thought
Emptied me of concerns and contentions. It disappeared too.

This planet a dream of butterflies
     waiting for winter. The next instant,
     life can leak from the universe
Empty forever.

Being is more finite than ever, as it may
     end in an instant, everywhere.
     This kind of change is too sudden to bear.
I become blind, deaf, dumb, dead inside, running for
my life.

How do the Powerful Men of our Era permit **tOTAL
tERROR**
     to grow unchecked, earth's cancer, needing
     commitments to health beyond the wits of
everyone.
To foresee catastrophe is not necessarily to step out
of the way.

     Are we just waiting?

Do **something** I tell myself and I start to sidle toward an
inkling of
what I *might* try to do.
Think of the alternatives. Hear the cries of babies. Smell
the fragrant
soil. Wait and listen. This earth cries out, hardly born and
gasping.
Shrieking for life. "Please don't throw me in the garbage."

We are all together, in pride, in selfishness, in stubborn-
ness. How infinitely sad the predicament of the self-righ-
teous. "Follow the one
True way or be damned forever. Follow me." I'm so very
sorry.

*Adam Atkin, Doctor of Neurophysiology, has been a medical
researcher in visual and brain sciences for 30 years. He has
published several books in his field.*

MEMORIAL DAY

On the street, dull green jeeps are rolling,
pickup trucks, divisions of veterans,
bellies extended, proud, as if
with child, are marching.

                              auxiliary women
are marching in high-heeled shoes,
under umbrellas, their purses
are hung on their arms,

                              the girls
from the Holy Name School are marching
in purple tights and Valkyrie helmets
with yellow braids,

                              and here on the corner
a boy with a toy soldier is shooting
his water pistol into the innocent rain.

*Martha Collins teaches creative writing at the University of
Massachusetts in Boston.*

Everywhere the absence of grace   Everywhere events
spiraling
Down   Everywhere anarchy, everywhere mass disasters
Everywhere the air rolling in surges   Everywhere the
sacrament
Of rage   Everywhere echoes unknown before   Every-
where the fist
Everywhere the savagery, the drowning of mind   Every-
where
The bones, everywhere the bullets   Everywhere the terror-
ist
Everywhere consciousness raked over and rearranged by
war
Everywhere the police, the politicians   Everywhere the
Republic
Of Lies   Everywhere lips parted, broken, bruised, blue
Everywhere the awareness of tragedy   Everywhere waking
To find blood on the pillow case   Everywhere
The bitter toxic medicinal salts   Everywhere the chronic
cough
Everywhere the plague workers   Everywhere the cremato-
rium
Everywhere stiffening skin, staring eyes, gaping mouths
Everywhere

*John Gilgun is a Professor of English at Missouri Western College
in St. Jo, Missouri.*

IV

Recent American Wars

Vietnam

AN OBSCENITY

You know the war well,
It was all over the tube:
Sounds, scenes, broken bodies,
Death, destruction, devastation,
A terrible, cruel and gruesome fight.
We took it for ten years;
They held on for thirty.
Here's a scene you never saw.
It's heap big chief general
Fresh out of his PX comfort
Come to the front to inspire
His loyal troops, to encourage
Them to keep fighting, Gung-Ho.
He is in his air conditioned
Sparkling command car.
It's so hot and humid
The windows fog up completely.
Four grunts run along side
Wiping off the window fog
And their sweat;
Poor bastard, never saw much.

Stan Proper, a native New Englander, lives with his wife and son in Concord, Massachusetts. His concern is with political, social, and environmental issues.

I WILL REMEMBER

I was too young
much too young

to wade through dense sauna jungles
to hike waist-deep in mined rice paddies
to sleep with one eye open
to shovel my buddies into garbage bags
to take a cold, steel rifle for a lover
to slaughter a people I did not know
         in a land where I did not belong
to see villages burned in the name of liberation
to fear a snapping twig in the night air
to take shrapnel from friendly fire
to search and destroy
to taste napalm clinging to the morning breeze

the roar of ever-present evacuation choppers
the sparse chattering of constant gunfire
the sticky dampness of raining orange defoliant
the whine of a transistor radio now and then
the grizzly inventory of daily body counts
the distant hammering of heavy artillery
the stiff stench of drying American blood
the enemy bodies stacked like firewood
the dirty children dying in the streets
the Vietnamese girls working for American dollars

I was too young—but I will remember
                I will remember . . .

Carl Eugene Moore is President and CEO of a company manufac-
turing battery conditioners for computer battery packs. He lives
and writes in Newberry, South Carolina.

TAKING SIDES

The bravest of my generation
were shot down in Vietnam.
As assassinations rocked
America I was left to
napalm death and body counts
on the six o'clock news,
choking on dinner.
Motown moved me
the Beatles soothed me
and white buckskin cowgirl
Janis Joplin dead of drugs,
and the brilliant Hendrix,
dead of drugs. Fear and
anger turned to rioting
in Chicago where police
cracked heads and dropped
tear gas. The country cried.
Protegés of Thomas Szasz
had nervous breakdowns
returning to the heavy streets
as hippies and gurus while
17 year-old Marine door-gunners
came home insane.

Donna Dulfon pursues her part-time accounting career in Massapequa, New York.

VIETNAM IN '69

A score of years ago
I was sent to a second-hand war
created by second-rate leaders
which destroyed first-rate lives
of soldiers and civilians unfairly
placed on the path of political dice,
loaded dice, in a craps game which
should never have begun,
and now I know
spiritual wounds licked clean,
still scar.

Rod Farmer has been a farm laborer, dump truck driver, grocery store clerk, and a soldier in Vietnam. Now a Professor of Education and History in Farmington, Maine, he is overjoyed that the Cold War is over.

SERVICE

Always killing ourselves—the earth
sucks up blood so fast, stains remain
only in our minds. Sometimes sanity demurs,
sits out of range, wrapped in shriveled
wings like a stunned gargoyle.

Dealing with it at twenty-five, I saw
a grown man fish for squirrels below
the surgeon general's window. We discarded
uniforms for hospital blues, for—we thought—
a form of truth.

Here, the doctor captain rode a bicycle
calmly through our castles of terror, nodded
at our flight to bars, ducked chairs sailing
through the thick ward air, ignored dead soldiers
of thunderbird smashed into green pieces
on the bathroom floor.

At night, I listened to a very private private
who murdered his C.O. for probably no good reason
at all, who said he also killed his father
every night before jerking off into dreams, always
of lifeless birds raining black down
from the heavens, he sobbing to revelations

That we were either soldiers or maladaptives
with stunted character, deformed behavior,
or neurophysical imbalances. Our skeletons
were hauled out of closets, called to attention,
rudely inspected and redressed in new clothes.

Cured, headbones rewired to carry our ration
of guilt, we marched back into service
with picket fence papers, or exited silently
onto tranquilized sofas to watch unfold black
and white adventures at Mai Lai and Kesanh, waiting

With the nervous politicians for the others to return,
the others with eyes of smoldering coaltown seams,
words blazing like torched prairie grass, their silent
wounds spilling red letters—the old unspeakable
alphabet, useful for one more page of history.

*Homer Mitchell is an adjunct instructor in a prison, just received
an MFA from Goddard College, Vermont, grows herbs, and
photographs nature.*

WHAT MY NEIGHBOR BEN SAID

I saw them hanging there,
fruit on Martian trees.
Hand grenades on wires from limbs,
still, moist, like figs.
My squad paced off its fate.
A tank lurched, the wire tripped,
the air spun with flame.
Trees flung their happy fruit.
My friend's head crashed off,
neck a tangled mess of ribbons in the grass,
red, yellow, like the ones in my sister's drawer.
The tank rolled over mute, an old rhino.

I pry the gun from my dead one
to stalk, toot, fire to the empty click.
Buddies pin me down, tie me up,
stroke my cheek with a muzzle—
carry me back to the U.S.S. Hope.
And just like that I got off a plane,
from Saigon to Long Beach in a day.
A general slips me 100 dollars,
and says good-job-well-done-welcome-home
I smacked the bill to his chest—
Stuck to his medals, flapping in the wind,
the little gray flag to my fear—
Stick it up your khaki ass I said.

I roll my reefers, now, at sunrise,
string my lines with weights,
the best bass fisherman in Cedar Lake.
But would you take me, Bill, to Ivy Tech?
I need a new trade . . . I can't sleep.
You see I've cleaned out whole families,
but I can't find a place.

W.K. Buckley is an Associate Professor of English at Indiana
University. He lives in Gary.

WAR WAS DIFFERENT THEN:
Unwritten Notes to a Brother
Who (Almost) Came Back from the War

1.

You laughed at me because I was weaker
and couldn't hit balls far or climb trees high,
but against Grandpa's dusty, heavy-lidded trunk
with cracked leather straps and blood-rust nails,
we pooled our strength and triumphed,
marveling fresh in hero-hordes
snatched for an old man's glory.
You and I together, culprit children more than once,
failures apart, movers in unison.
I couldn't go with you to the jungle,
being neither strong nor male,
but I sweated and ached and shook with you
and helped you lift the lid
to gather vague spoils of a different war.

2.

Straining young bodies across a sharp edge,
blood rush foreheadward,
we tugged souvenirs from enticing snarls
of dull-colored clutter and knots.
Helmet, medal, knife case, snapshot—
mother-henned props for tales of planned moves—
thrust intact to eager palms where grateful wives
slapped them alive and wrapped them in cloth.
I wonder if you thought of Grandpa's horde
as you hid-and-sought in murky heat.
From among sharp grasses and sponge-bladed weeds,
you, too, sent souvenirs to swaddle and deeply inter,
to tempt the imagination-craving of unborn young
and leave them famished.

3.

Grandpa's scraped helmet with glance-bullet sides
that served his purpose and saved his breath
swallowed your six-year-old head,
but you refused to enter mock-battle otherwise clad
and let if fall over your pellucid eyes,
so obstructing your view that you peppered blind shots
at anonymous faces on unseen ground
to punish half-defined sins.
Your own helmet must have fit better,
clearing your vision for who and where and why.
But the protection was so tight
that it squeezed the logic from your brain,
freeing it to dribble the matted growth
until you joined it there.

4.

With pudgy fingers you caught the medal,
dragging it eel-like from a puddle of charms,
not caring that it was tarnished
or that you couldn't read its stiff syllables
or understand what currency had bought it.
It was merely a bauble to pin on your shirt,
dangle from your pocket, clutch in your mitten.
You never examined the mint-new medal
your own courage purchased from a rack of gifts
designed to debrief a conscience.
You saw only voids when they pinned it to your chest,
your limbs locked in some "At-ten-tion!"
that I couldn't hear though I strained,
that you couldn't explain through the mist.

5.

Strikingly barren without its metal mate,
the knife case was bewitching still,
the raised grain of the aging leather
stirring tiny fingers, awakening touch.

The insignia was foreign, yet magic and strange,
conjuring visions of hot teeming squares,
of unfamiliar aliments and ancient rooms.
Armed with the case, you nulled a myriad colossals.
I wonder if you could have freed yourself
had I dashed screaming to the earth's dim edge
and laid it in your grasping hands.
I wonder, too, if your own case was filled
as you prowled and foraged among weeping vines
or if, in the end, you resorted to fangs and claws.

6.

The slice of celebrated stone-rough monument
was too slim for proper recognition,
but Grandpa smiled with his bosom pal,
their shoulders Siamese-mingled.
Though all but those rose-flesh arcs had faded,
pride shone through the glossless paper,
engulfing us in tingles that never grew stale.
But your own picture radiated terror
that was rushed, too pushed for sights and markers.
I echoed with your lack of lines, frown or smile.
When I heard that you had shed your reason
somewhere between the bars of a bamboo cage,
too late I came to your blank white cell,
to your wiped-slate face and steady stare.

Allison Wilson is an Associate Professor of English living in Jackson, Mississippi.

BODY COUNT: THE DEAD AT TAY NINH

They had no place to put them
so they piled them, boots
pointed skyward by the mess tent.
And still they kept on coming.
Choppers brought dead and wounded
in all day. One man ran
out from a swirl of dust,
his severed arm in hand,
he staggered over and sat
for two whole minutes before
he realized where he was.
And still they kept on coming.
Like pilgrims, the sick and lame
who missed the ships came to gaze
in disbelief. Bodies so close
together the lies came easy.
They slept, they weren't
really dead. They'd wake
up when the war was over.
This was it for them.
No more bullshit sir.
From now on, just think
of us as dead.
But by dusk the last ones
came from the Angel Plain;
the grass had caught on fire.
Their bodies black and crisp
curled in the purple light
as if begging for the release
they knew would never come.
At dawn, they flew them out
in bags, mopped up the mess
for chow.

Kevin Bowen served in Vietnam as a radio operator with the First Cavalry Division. He is Co-Director of the William Joiner Center for the Study of War and Social Consequences. He has returned to Vietnam several times initiating exchanges.

PROGNOSIS: GUARDED

He denies hallucinations,
but does have flashbacks:
the edge of a village, near Saigon,
something moves in the long grass.

This Christmas while shopping
he saw some Vietnamese and wanted to choke them.
At home he had thoughts
of throwing his children through windows.

Quietly, almost inaudibly,
he says he's had a temper
since being raped, right before discharge,
by a commanding officer.

He knows today's date, the time;
he can spell "world" backwards;
he can list the Presidents since Kennedy,
though he skips President Johnson.

Kevin FitzPatrick has been a postal clerk, ice-cube factory worker, park groundskeeper, bartender, crime researcher, self-defense instructor, job developer, sports director, claims examiner, and editor of The Lake Street Review since 1977.

A LESSON IN CAPITALISM

The cherry Lieutenant called in a barrage of Willy Peter.
The shells fell a hundred yards short, white
tentacles of phosphorus. Cohen, who wasn't
the son of no Jewish banker, was impaled
by burning liquid. I shot him up with morphine,
screams coming from the holes in his stomach,
the tips of all his fingers on fire. Again,
I was in that landscape by Hieronymus Bosch,
the Lieutenant squatting in a drainage ditch
of shit and Agent Orange, shivering, crying,
holding his ears. Cohen's pain bells of fire.
A former college boy, an Econ major from Indiana
the officer didn't know the shells fell short
because the munitions maker kept back
an ounce of powder to save a buck.
After all, we were only grunts
in a jungle sweat shop,
the whole fucking war the ninth floor
of the Triangle Shirt Waist Factory.

▌ *Elliot Richman lives and writes in Plattsburgh, New York.*

A WINTER'S NIGHT IN PHU BAI*

Across the coarse burlap
security blanket of sandbags
I watch
the whisper tendrils
of ground fog
silently slide over the wire
holding blood dripping fangs
of shadow dancing
boyhood nightmares
magnified
a thousandfold.

I can't remember which is
more fearsome,
the dying or the killing.

*Phu Bai: a Vietnamese hamlet a few miles south of Hue known
primarily for its graveyards.

*John C. Muir is a disabled combat veteran of the Vietnam War
whose harrowing 13 month tour of duty appears in detail in
Everything We Had (Random House, 1981. Nominated for the
Pulitzer Prize.)*

NAM

He was a stranger,
    now he is my brother.

We are here in a strange land bound together
    by fear.
The enemy is advancing;
We listen to the shelling and wonder if we'll
    make it this time.

A foreign bullet found his thigh.
I tore cloth from his pants and made a tourniquet.

He cried in my arms,
    and we waited . . .

Pat Brodnicki is a 52 year old wife and the mother of three grown sons. She is also a teacher and a tutor in Niantic, Illinois.

DRAWING FIRE

Imagine snakes underfoot
fields of ten foot buffalo grass
sharp as the razor in a street lord's
shoe the dung-baking Asian sun
canvas boots slopping through
mud dressed in quicklime
rock and country music pulsing in ears
sharpened by the whine of the biggest
fucking bugs you ever saw and
birds droning away hidden inside galaxies
of green; that, and the effacing
speech-slurring slide of grease on
an unseen river, a few huts left empty
in suddenly falling afternoon rain
and you get the idea
                        it's called you are bait
call us when you draw the fire
looks better on the HQ chart
with arrows this way and that
stalking red line where the jet fighters
screech in for napalm bursts and
the Black Pony gunships burden
the dazzled water with metal and sulphur
American hail and the skulking VC
take it among the leaves only
given away by the flash of burning
fat and exploding powder.

Except when the fat and powder was us
and the fire came too quick to dance
around and the red body parts of
baseball-playing kids from places in
Delaware and Wisconsin dissolved,
abstract swatches in the yellow air.

Michael Shorb writes and edits technical material dealing with computer software, hardware, and the telecommunications industry. He also writes about historical and environmental issues.

VIETNAM MORATORIUM

They are reading the dead, are reading
The names of the dead in battle tonight
On the soaked cement in one lone spotlight
But mainly in candlelight and under the war black
Umbrellas they read the names of Hope Hopmann
Johns Janssen the list they read
Is sick with moisture the microphone
Coughs with the weather and the people
Stand listen do not talk but remember
The dead on the side of the world remote
From this wet small place where the eyes
Stare down at the Wagners Watkins Yates Young dead
On the public address tonight as
They read the dead.

Richard Swanson teaches English at Madison Area Technical College in Wisconsin.

WHEN YOU BREAK SOMETHING VERY NEAR TO YOUR SOUL
THE ECHO WHISTLES IN YOUR BRAIN
LIKE MORTAR SHELLS FALLING ON DANANG

Shell shock.
It's the military term for active neurosis.
But the army never whispers
to the fresh, young infantry
just on line from Peoria, Topeka or San Diego
about the awful nights of shelling or the way
blood spurts out of bodies with an arm torn off.
And then your buddy's eyes, the way they turn
and grope for God, the way his fingers grope
for cigarettes . . .
And the army never hints the war
may not be worth your bloody shirt,
the crucifix above your woman's bed,
the soldiers that have died already
stinking in the flooded paddies groaning
from the weight of death,
forests dying by the countryful and kids
that thrust a baby at you so you'll kiss
its dynamite infested sickness;
the sweat, the drugs, the pain, the fury.

And finally, when your eyes have scarred
enough to keep the sight of dying out;
when your nose becomes immune to burning flesh,
your ears to women screaming
through nights of violation

you're sent home
to Illinois or Kansas or the coast
where children hide in bushes
pointing stick-guns at each other
playing war.

And you watch,
and you watch.

Nothing makes sense. All around you
is an echo like the bombs at Da Nang.

Even children carry knives to cut your heart.

Craig Crist-Evans teaches creative process of personal mythology to kids. He lives on a small ranch surrounded by the Sangre de Cristo and San Juan Mountains in Denver, Colorado.

R & R

In 1969 my nineteen-year old husband of five months
Went to War. He really had no desire to kill
Anyone, nor did he have any idea what that conflict
Was all about. No one did then. But I was pregnant
And the army offered Benefits and Training, and, well,
We were young and naive. He played sax and
Flute in the Third Army Band, marching at ceremonies,
Spit and polished. In Vietnam he serenaded
Villagers while their leaders were interrogated,
Shot and thrown into mass burial pits.
A man of conscience, he did what he could:
He went insane.

In horrible letters with writing all ragged,
He described waking up to find himself wandering
Around the compound, shells going off
In the distance and inside his head. He was
Crying and couldn't stop. Finally he turned
To marijuana and yoga and shades, so he
Wouldn't have to see and feel.

That September we met in Oahu, tourist print shirts
Disguising our lust. We slept on beaches,
In pineapple groves, and sailed a three-masted
Barque to Diamond Head. It was kind of like a
Disneyland for soldiers. At night he was mute.
Jumping off rocks, I played a game: how far could I fall
Without taking a breath? If I died, would he be spared?

Helpless, he held me until the hotel lights
Reflected in the water danced like fireflies in a floor show,
Then changed to goldfish on parade, alchemy of midnight highs,
Our love unable to leap the chasm of separate realities,
Warm rain unable to heal our wounds.
Later I miscarried. He is still on Stelazine.

*Lynn Carrigan is a clinical social worker in a university public
hospital, a social and political activist and optimistic about our
evolution away from violence.*

A MEDIC RECALLS A GRUNT

That soldier was a loner, liked a book,
And never got loquacious when he drank.
Like all the others had a distant look,
And like the others all his clothing stank.
He'd come to me with ringworm or some bruise,
Had one trick knee, but wouldn't wear a brace,
Complained about how Bravo got the screws
'Cause Bravo never spent much time in base.
He really was too new for me to know
By name or town, or if his girl was pretty,
Or what he thought about when feeling low,
Or how he came to be in Cu Chi City.
Today I took a leak down by the knoll
And found him, trussed and headless, in a hole.

*Stephen Sossaman, Vietnam Veteran, founded Veteran's Civic
Action Team in response to the Gulf War.*

THE VET WHO NEVER LEFT NAM

"The way out is through
the door," the Army psychiatrist
told him. So he smashed
his way through and slept
with a shotgun on his
chest, till they took him
to the hospital.
  "The longest journey
begins with a single step,"
he told the doctor there, staring
at the place where his feet
had been.

Donald Caswell is the Publications Coordinator for the International Brotherhood of Boilermakers in Prairie Village, Kansas.

nichols park

our plan was to meet here
when the vietnam war was over
in the heart of winter I return alone
skaters blades scar the ponds surface
and the ferris wheel
is an unmovable gawk
in summer I rode that ferris wheel
with a girlfriend
up into julys fireworks
the wheels lights spinning
like neon tracer bullets in the dark
where have the young dead gone
in this grim winter
the only visual sign is a word
a name eli eli bridge company
riveted to a crossbar on the wheel
I start for a moment
at the tree a memorial for him
when I enter the pavilion
a cracked ballroom mirror turns
on the ceiling
throwing violent light

*Victor Pearn lives with his two daughters in Boulder, Colorado,
where he teaches and edits poetry for "Red Dirt."*

REMEMBERING FROM THE GRAVE

Young John began Camelot to such a cheer.
Started the Peace Corps. Hope.
After that got his brains splattered all over Dallas.

I lost mine in The Nam in '68
though I'm not on THE WALL because my body survived,
kept alive like some ghoulish corpse on hospital machines.

When Martin took the hate bullet for talking love
your brother, man, I began to study history at the
university, as though I hadn't had enough of its stench.
But I didn't know I was dead.

They gave my body a degree; said I could "teach"
I took the body to a factory instead.
Needed the dead job for the dead head.
Been rotting there ever since.

These days my wife's leaving
taking the kids, selling the house.
Says I won't talk to her anymore.
I can't tell her dead men don't talk.

*Gary Goude is a machinist and a Vietnam vet. He was actively
opposed to the Persian Gulf War.*

AFTER THE FALL OF SAIGON

Jim has nightmares,
and because of this
Cathy is afraid to sleep.
He won't see a doctor,
so she has been going
for most of fifteen years.
Sometimes she lies
awake and can see faces
he has told her about:
the old woman who might have
been no more than thirty;
the man, at least sixty.
It is their eyes
that disturb her most;
no hate nor even anger.
They are not vacant either.
That's what she would have
expected. But in that dark
is death, and nothing
she can say
could make them cry.
She will never understand
how he can sleep.

Louis McKee lives and teaches in Philadelphia, Pennsylvania.

We Speak for Peace

FROM NAM TO ARMAGEDDON

At the IND entrance on the busy corner
he sits on the sidewalk
jeans rolled up to show his stumps
one just below the knee
and one at the ankle
tapering like a leg o' lamb
the shrapnel-pocked flesh
devoid of muscle and pale as dough
begging for his daily bread.
The torn carton panel in his lap
reads, "VIETNAM VET."

In sun or sleet he sits at that corner
greeting every passerby.
Even a dime in his cup calls forth
a hearty "God bless you, buddy!"
or a heartfelt "Have a nice day, lady!"
Yet his sunken brown dark-circled eyes
and his brown-bearded Semitic features
recall the Man of Sorrows
whose own stigmata sting no worse.

Beside him on the sidewalk
rest shiny plastic prostheses like doll parts,
their flesh-colored enamel
looking just as false as dolls' flesh.
They'd played no part of him
till his true limbs lighted on a mine near Pleiku
and blew his pins out from under him for good.
"It blew my mind out too," he said—
the pain and then the drugs
more pain and then more drugs—
"but I'm clean now that I'm reborn."

In winter even thermal wear can't halt
the chill that climbs his spine from the sidewalk
and wracks his ribs and pierces his lungs
like shrapnel, till staph infects his stumps

whose chronic bleeding adds insult to in-
justice, and pneumonia saps his strength.
The VA hospital then becomes his post
till gaunt, eyes newly haunted,
he reclaims his corner.

He reclaims his corner of the world
the week America begins to bomb Iraq.
He says, "I hate to see it start
but this time only one thing counts:
when they come back, treat the vets right.
When we came back, and you went into a bar
and said you was in Nam, they'd call you baby-
killer and try to pick a fight.
Yeah, this time treat vets right.

"But this time it's gonna go nucular.
I know, 'cause last year I found the Lord
and read it in the Book—
this time it's gonna be Armageddon—take a look.
It's in Isaiah 13.6.
Check out Ezekiel, Daniel, Zechariah—
they all lead up to Revelation.
These are the last days
the Lord be praised.

"God bless you, buddy, and have a nice day!"

*George Held teaches at Queens College, New York, and is at
work on a novel based on his three years in Czechoslovakia.*

Vietnam War Memorial Wall

DEDICATION OF THE WAR MEMORIAL

Three priests stand before microphones
against a sky of stone, reading
from Samuel, then praying.
Black crèpe encircles
the platform like a modest skirt.

They clasp their hands
ceremoniously and prayers fly
as if on new wings to alight
in the uppermost leaves of the oaks,
bending the branches so they seem

to be stirred by wind.
But the air is cool, still,
enfolding us like a stiff embrace.
It is time, time to begin
reading the names.

Volunteers stand ready
to take their turns.
Gulls fly overhead, crying out.
Bobby Lee Able, Charles Edward
Able, David Anthony Able,
Frank Wayne Able, Jim Farrell
Able, and on through
the Ables until the last
daylight breaks a hole
in the sky and seeps over

the faces of the crowd.
The reader is still in the a's.
A boy plays in the distance,
his red shirt the exact red
of the flag hanging over

the platform where the next
reader now stands and reads

from the list, an unbroken
scroll stored in boxes and boxes
hidden by the platform's skirts.

Babies have started to cry
and children play swing
the statue striking graceful
poses at first, but as
the darkness crawls from here

and there on hands and knees,
they imitate these bunch-backed forms of night.
Mothers have folded babies
into the cool grass.

How much longer? someone
unseen whispers.
But we are still
in the a's.
A small tongue of flame

rises near the reader's
head and the crowd gasps
in one voice
at this burst
of holy fire.

The names
are no longer familiar:
Abeyta, Abo, Adelman,
Agostini, Ahmed, Aikawa,
Ajisaka, Akimota, Aw.

Someone must stop her
or we will be here forever.

Eleanor Swanson teaches, lives, and writes in Lakewood, Colorado. She is also active in the Rocky Mountain Peace Center in Boulder.

VIETNAM MEMORIAL

When you visit the wall to locate
a name, you must know the date
of casualty, or else consult a well-used book
at the entrance which tells where to look.

Like still bodies of water the top lies even.
From shallow to deep to shallow again,
the monument slopes into the ground,
as if with involvement everyone drowned.

When you walk in you read who was the first
one to die and, leaving, the last, feel immersed
in the center as you walk down the path,
see yourself mirrored in a dark glass.

Why not put up a statue? critics contended.
Each soldier was a hero who defended
his country. Why this headstone dug in the heart
of a city of eighteenth-century art?

Go ask the designer who created a park
and left us a body count on the dark
wall, silent roll call of a war,
that keeps you asking what it was they died for.
Go ask the sculptor who chiseled names
of fifty-eight thousand on black granite frames,
letters that make people cry as they trace.
Go ask the builder who heaved those stones into place.

Deborah Fleming is an academic counselor at Ohio State University. She rides horses and climbs mountains.

THE WALL BETWEEN THE NAMES

I don't know if you ever noticed but if you stand at the base of the wall at the apex when it's quiet you can feel a warmth . . . it's as if you're being surrounded by all the spirits of the wall. (The last Firebase)

Deep in this masculine scar,
black as telegram ink,
there are boys and girls
waiting for news,

sons who think
they see the faces
of their fathers
in the granite,

pointing to the ashen names,
as if pointing
to a bruised shin
or stubbed toe,

the pre-dawn muster
of fatigue jackets, watches
set to Saigon time . . . Midnight
when the mortars fell,

and the moon, the same moon
over Kansas, New York,
and California lost,
shivering in the factory smoke
driven to the ground.

Lonnie Hodge is a therapist and clinical director at Amethyst Hospital in Charlotte, North Carolina. He was an Ordnance Officer in the U.S. Army.

VISITING THE VIETNAM VETERANS MEMORIAL

A long black corner,
each end ascending slowly
from the earth.

Two triangles touching
in the middle,
its zenith of death.

Name after name
telegraphs letters
like white lace at attention
on this wall of night.

They come as sleep-walkers,
each visitor a quiet loss.

They lay at the base
roses, letters, miniature flags.

They touch names,
fragments of sons and daughters.

Like the rain of stars
we are wet with infinite tears.

We are hot puddles on cobblestones.

*Joseph Gustafson teaches English in Worcester Public Schools.
He has been writing and publishing his poetry for 20 years.*

CONSTRUCTION/VIETNAM MEMORIAL, 1991

February rain dissolves winter, as the back-hoe genuflects
& cuts deep into the frozen Courthouse lawn. This scarring

is the newest testament in a Square already relic cluttered,
as deep & divisive as the war it represents. Cold embraces,

rain touches my neck and I shiver, silently spilling tears
as I watch the grass I played on torn apart, another casualty

to war. And I remember. Bruce's desperate voice
while we sat homegrown-stoned over euchre. 1969.

He was 19 and already lost, as memories bled out from him:
his Vietnamese Wife & the comfort of her father's silk-

pillowed opium den, their dark-haired baby solemn & pale-
eyed
staring back from the crackled snapshot Bruce cradled

in his wide coarse palm. He had no words for the war itself,
only for the fragile sweetness found & lost there.

But his scarred hands, stained and shaking as they caressed
the small square photo, silently shaped the war for me.

We brought the boys home, but it didn't end. Bruce
danced faster and faster. To forget. To remember. Wintered

without spring through 20 years of 'luudes & reds, washed
back with Jack Daniel's, till he finally crashed through

to another plane on the midnight span of the Spencer bridge.
There were others.

But his broken life was the fist that smacked me, shattered
the last of my illusions, cursed me with vision

so sharp that now, I have to turn away down my own
icy street. To remember. To forget.

*Beth Kelley interviews clients with sexually transmitted diseases
for the Indiana State Department of Health. She lives with her
two wonderfully active pacifist children in Bloomington.*

Central American Wars

GRENADA, LIBYA, NICARAGUA, SALVADOR, PANAMA, ETC.

The sky looks harmless and the grass
beams up all around,
but a tendon has been cut in the arm of God.

This is the first day in the week of a new age.
Somewhere a bird flaps unevenly away.

The face of an airman zooms and resumes:
"This is great. This is what it's all about."

Under the smooth surface of the canal
the water is full of cadavers.
Alligators have moved out;
even the buzzards refuse their food.

Only yellow sulfurs don't know
how the upper air begins to thin.

Last night the moon rocked and tumbled,
only it was the blue earth.

The devil shakes hands at the airport.
"How you doing?"
"Great. This is what it's all about."

*Justine Buisson conducts workshops, works in a library, and
actively seeks peace in Pax Christi Movement in Miami, Florida.
She has traveled widely and continues to do so.*

Recent American Wars

BLOSSOMS

(for Suyapa Gutierrez, 1980-1984, killed by a
contra mortar shell outside her home in
Teotecacente, Nicaragua)

My four-year-old daughter could
play with the camellia blossoms
half the day, and does. While I
sit beside her, reading of Suyapa
Gutierrez, four years old, blown
to bits outside her own front door,
Emma counts camellias into a tub,
then chants the numbers back to me,
demanding praise. I read how
Suyapa's mother planted flowers where
the bomb exploded. Emma is making
families of blossoms now, the larger
ones parents, the smaller, fragile
ones, the children. <u>Watch me!</u> she cries
and gathers them in armfuls, straightens,
spins. She spins, and scarlet rains
upon the grass, splashed with sunlight
and transmuted by it to something liquid,
ominous. I put out my hand and stop
her dance. As evening shadows creep
beneath the trees, Emma sings softly,
safe beside me: her ribs stir like
small birds beneath my encircling
hands.

Rebecca Baggett writes and publishes poems, short stories, and essays. She lives with her family in Albany, Georgia.

THE WOMAN FROM GUATEMALA

Sometimes when I cannot fall asleep
I think about a woman from Guatemala
who never left Guatemala while she was alive
but when she was dead made the news,
which is how I came to know her on "Sixty Minutes."
She was 26 years old, a law student,
when one day she was pulled from a cab,
her throat slit, her hands chopped off,
her body tortured till her heart stopped, and after.
It is ridiculous to think that her spirit
just slipped away as suddenly as the first blow,
impossible to think about her resting in peace.
I don't; what I think about when my mind is stuck
on making sense of why the janitor at my grammar school
molested little girls, is this woman from Guatemala,
whose naked body was selected out of a morgueful,
her hands propped on her breasts,
so photographers could film her to make a point,
just as the ones who murdered her
had murdered her to make a point.
We are as different as night and day, she and I.
I, for one thing, am alive, which is how
sometimes my insomnia leads me to think of her
instead of counting sheep to fall asleep.
These nights, I imagine she is just as dead,
only her hands are attached again to her arms
and clasping a single white rose against the
soft white cotton of a hand-woven shroud
Indian women made for their sister.
She is lying in a coffin, and her hair is combed.
Other times, I see her mutilated body,
and that image becomes the prototype of a mutilation
against which no other will ever measure up

*Felicia Mitchell teaches creative writing at Emory and Henry
College in Emory, Virginia.*

JUST CAUSE

Outside the black fences of the cemetery
on a hill near Panama City
lies a field wild with flowers and grasses
but for a tract of dirt
and upturned stems and leaves torn, curled,
mottled by tropical storms,
where one small woman stoops, kneels,
unfurls a spool of thread
round twigs pegged quadrangularly.

She has followed the grid and guesses
given her by the Yankee colonel
who said he thinks he knows now
most names of the hundred-forty or so
civilians consigned quickly
in the heat for prophylaxis
in the mopping-up.

She leaves an orchid
to celebrate his heart,
her rosary
where she sees his hands,
a baseball cap
embroidered Tomas
at the head of the grave.

She stakes a claim
for mourning.

*Although he has taught at high schools and colleges in New York
and Michigan, James W. Penha prefers his expatriate existence
in Asia where he is Director of Academic Advising for CUNY-
Lehman's Hiroshima, Japan campus.*

Recent American Wars

The Persian Gulf War of 1991

THE PERSIAN GULF WAR

I still breathe the gas of Auschwitz,
Feel Hiroshima ash all over my skin.

My children turned to LSD and heroin.
Rock music helped them drown out sounds.
They needed a cause, chose civil rights.
At times they marched to glory;
Sometimes they burned and looted.

My children lost faith in authority
When the U.S. President resigned.
But causes were still important—
Vietnam, hunger, AIDS.

Now my children are preventing WW III
By arresting aggression at the start
So the wheels of industry remain oiled.

Lena London Charney is a retired educator and administrator.
She loves to travel and has been to every continent except Antarc-
tica.

HOW TO USE THE U.N.

Ignore it
till it says what you want.
Then, Desert Shield and
sword in hand,
champion
its high principles.

Brian Daldorph is an Assistant Professor of English at the University of Kansas, Lawrence. He is also the Editor of "Coal City Review," and a long time member of Amnesty International.

YOUR NATIVE LAND

There is something in this native land business and you
cannot get away from it, in peace time you do not seem to
notice it much particularly when you live in foreign parts
but when there is a war and you are all alone and completely cut off from knowing about your country well then
there it is, your native land is your native land, it certainly
is.

Gertrude Stein

"A lot of people misunderstood how much of the population
believes" in the Ba'ath party "and how much of the opposition is dead . . ."

Senior U.S. government official quoted in an *International Herald Tribune* story, "Hussein's Grip is Stronger
Now."

The night before the deadline
for the Gulf War, watching Italian tv,
the reporter in Baghdad
asking how he'd talk with his bureau
when tomorrow the skies would be closed.
Later, the skies opened, dropping black rain, clouds seeded
with oil.

Nights under the covers, against the cold winter damp of
Tunisian stone
unheated homes. Short-wave junkie,
earphone jack mainlining the news.
Listening for protest marches
in the States, hearing yellow ribbons
for the troops instead.
The streets outside my window
too quiet. Not even
one barking dog. Waking to find

the jack still in my ear, the batteries
blinking. What did they say in *Brave New World* about
sleep learning?
That you never forget.

What's worse than war is how
we give up under it. The BBC goes back
to airing soccer. The bakeries open.
The war continues. That's how
they get away with it.
This old world order that has
such Calibans.

What we forget in peace comes home.
And drives us there, to say
this opposition is not dead.

*Sibyl James has taught English in the U.S., China and Mexico.
She has just returned after two years as a Fulbright professor of
literature in Tunis, Tunisia.*

WE WERE WATCHING THE WHEEL OF FORTUNE WHEN
THE WAR CAME ON

The t.v. was flickering
and we were bickering
about what show to watch
but in the middle of "Wheel of Fortune"
suddenly the war
came on the tube:
the famous t.v. anchor
was interrupting
the program in progress
with news of the war,
and we were watching
the instant replay
of the first
shrill whistle
of the first IBM missile,
of the first
ratatattat
of the big guns:
we were watching the live camera action
of the first news briefing
of the first furrowed brow
of the first general:
we were watching to see
the unquivering chin
of the secretary of defense
and the stern faced president:
we were watching the whole
company get on
with the show:
there on the screen
we were watching all evening
looking into our t.v.
like a window,
sitting comfortably
in our recliner arm chairs

Recent American Wars

popping some popcorn
cracking a beer
watching the war
hoping to get a peek
at the enemy,
wishing to see
the whites of their eyes
wanting some blood—
just a little—
though we knew
if watching the war
got too much
we could turn
the damned thing off,
with just a touch
of our remote control
if the going got
too rough.

Phillip Miller marched in protest against the Vietnam War in the '70s. He lives, writes and teaches English in Kansas City, Missouri.

FOUR O'CLOCK, JANUARY 15, 1991

In the mailroom the young men talk of war
And listen to television news reports
They swagger in tight T-shirts
All muscle and bravado that fail to hide
A darkness trembling
Behind their eyes

Fragile peace pinioned by held breaths
The day yields in ticking measure
Everyone is full of theories
Talk drifts like milkweed in wind
Stirring everywhere
Settling nothing

A roaring sound rends the night
As a beast long-dead wakes
Uncoils from rusted sleep
A machine-oiled zephyr whispers hot
The time is now
Our cause is just

Did we not stand here recent days
While grown men fought tears
Ran fingertips
Across marble etched with names
memories engraved with faces
Monuments to the dead

Twenty years and we've fast forgotten
How easily our leaders lie
How meaningless it was then
How dust dulls past and pain
Until innocence reformed
Is lost again

*Diana Smith was formerly a Reporter for the Associated Press.
She is now Editor of the College Press Service, a news service for
college newspapers.*

AS USUAL

At the dentist's office, teeth are being drilled.
Police patrol their designated streets.
We are instructed to have a good day
by cashiers at each market place.
Radios blare, horns honk, balloons burst,
clocks chime, classes convene. Trucks thunder
down highways. Traffic lights blink on and off.

Birds soar below shifting clouds. The surge
of life beneath dead grasses waits to be reborn.
A benign sun stares, swinging low
in a bland sky. Snow melts, tides rise and fall,
winds move lingering leaves. Flickers appear
and depart from feeders. Willows wave
languidly, refusing to change the color of their hair.

And half the world away missiles rise
swiftly in desert air. Bombs fall
with bruising regularity. Skies explode
altering landscapes forever. Sanity recedes,
hatreds flare. The cycle has come round
again, sending the world awry.

And I am sick with longing
for something elusive
called love.

Lyn Kozma, Registered Nurse, served in the Army Air Force in
World War II. Retired now, she reads, writes, and avidly
watches birds in West Islip, New York.

PAINT THE GUN DECKS RED

January 15th comes, passes, conflagration begins.
Bristling, missiled, bomb bloated warbirds shriek into dusk.
Predesignated targets, electronically sought, destroyed,
First to go, unwarned early warning radar.
Communications, central command soon follow.
Aged planned, youth manned sorties carry science aided
death
To a surprised, confused, naive enemy whose miscalcula-
tions
Discounted resolve. Fearfire rains down unceasingly
Renders the despot's yesterday's pride, today's rubble.
Billion dollar monuments to madness disintegrate, made
useless.
Airfields, bunkers, roads, bridges, launch sites, nuclear,
Chemical and biological capacities are reduced. Elite
troops,
Battle tested by a lesser enemy, face deathrain, die.
Weather hidden, unseen, unknown numbers of their dead
Litter the desert above and below the sand. Armored war
machines,
Once manned, once proudly paraded, now shattered
twisted burning
Wreckage, so too their human cargo. Enemy planes pru-
dently
Flee, avoid destruction, will intimidate another day.
Sky, sea cleared, the coalition soars and steams at will.
Exuberant pilots return, thumbs up and hailed, to go again.
Some are lost, next of kin, notified, mourn.
Others captured, brutally enemy displayed.
Euphoria reigns, dampened by random civilian targeted
enemy
Missiles. A desperate dictator faces Mecca, calls for the
Mother of battles. An apprehensive commander in chief
Seeks preacher comfort, speaks to religious broadcasters,
Deems his war just, calls for a day of prayer.
Viet Nam wary officer briefers, mosttimes amiable, some-
time

Hostile, spoonfeed sanitized communiqués to a regimented, docile,
Cowed, compliant, frustrated media. In Pentagonese, sorties,
Kills, MIAs, KIAs, POWs, EPWs, excursions and penetrations
Are enumerated. Questions parried with dont know, cant say,
Wont tell, classified, would aid the enemy, all accepted,
Relayed worldwide. War appears aseptic, remote, with
No Pain, no screams, no cries, no moans, no terror, no tears,
No blood, no guts, no burns, no triage, no amputations,
No faceless, no dismembered, no sightless, no mindless,
No carnage, no corpses, no stench, no shudders, no horror.
Today's leaders, like those past who captained the wooden
man-of-war, to mask the gore, to quell the squeamish,
Still paint the gun decks red.

Judge Daniel F. Spallone served in World War II. He has retired from the Connecticut Appellate Court and is now a State Trial Referee.

OLD GLORY

(Found poem from an ad in *The New York Times*, 2/91).

At Bloomingdale's
we're waving an olive branch
in one hand
Old Glory in the other.
It's possible
in fact preferable
to be peace-loving
and patriotic
at the same time.

We know watching
all that CNN
has got you swinging
between hope
and resignation,
so we've created just the thing.
Our Stars and Stripes Shop.

We'll buoy your spirits
with everything
from leather jackets
to beach towels
to mugs and more
all emblazoned
with Old Glory.

BATTLEFIELD GOOD LUCK CHARM

In the desert
a young soldier fingers
the red nylon panties
trimmed with black lace
his girl sent from back home.

It helps to know someone is waiting for you,
he says.
but it's embarrassing to wash them out
and so hard to keep them clean
in the huge dust bowl
that is Saudi Arabia.

Lisa Vice was born and raised in rural Indiana. She has been an unwed teenage mother, a welfare recipient, a file clerk, a nurse's aide, a farmer, a batik artist, a family planning counselor, and a mason's tender. She now teaches writing at Hunter College in New York City.

JANUARY 15, 1991

While a world waits,
The earth weeps,
And Heaven's torrential tears
Rain upon the graves of
Ghandi and King,
As if to cleanse from their woeful souls
Armageddon's time.

Elayne Clift is a social communications consultant, a writer, and a journalist. She lives in Maryland and travels far and wide.

AMERICAN WEDDING,
JANUARY 16, 1991

He will be a Good Provider.
He feeds us honeyed words
coating the throat
warm, thick,

he stalks deserts, jungles
where oily-tongued dark-bodied
enemies lurk,

he soothes us with tanks,
arsenal enough
to feed millions
(he is generous that way).

Now, on this day,
the dowry of our mind is delivered.
√ Flags fly like confetti.
We have married our fear.

Andrea Potos is an editor and program coordinator at the Wisconsin Academy of Sciences, Arts and Letters. She spends long hours riding her bike along the lake trails and dreaming up poems.

ECHOES

Under cover of darkness on a moonless night
U.S. fighter bombers have attacked Iraq.
Radio News Bulletin 1-16-91

I listen, stunned, and
like a dormant volcano
fifty year-old memories erupt;

unexpected tears well up;
I hear echoes of sirens,
gas mask drills, remember

talks of quick victory, dashed
by harsh reality—disillusion,
suffering, pain, death
lying in wait
        then as now.

Why, why, do stubborn macho men
        glory in gory war
                again and again?

*Ingrid Reti is committed to feminism, pacifism and environmental-
ism. She is a literature and creative writing instructor at California Polytechnic State University.*

IN THE LINE OF DUTY

Calloused fingers trace a weld of scar
on his shoulder. He remembers the war,
the polished politicos of a nation
espousing his duty
to underwrite the lives
of a generation being lost.

He remembers the bewildered, lost
look of men gaping at the scar
of war on the land, counting lives
of friends, of women and babies sacrificed to that war.
He hears the words "killed in the line of duty"
describing black rubber bags enroute to a griefless nation.

He sees LBJ storming that nation,
heralding the number of enemy lost,
proclaiming it the duty,
the right of America to remove the scar
of Communism from South Vietnam, to fight the war
against aggression, to fight to save lives.

He remembers scores of lives
blown apart in a distant nation—
boys not quite men, squandered in war
against an enemy lost
by day but returning to scar
the night with white-hot tracers of deadly duty.

Bush pounds the podium, talks of duty,
of America's resolve to protect innocent lives
from a madman. CNN anchors are silent as jets scar
the desert of a smoking, cratered nation.
There is brief mention of the number lost
in the first few days of war.

This is his third night watching the war,
the third night for flashes of guard duty,
for mental slideshows of faces lost,
for whitened knuckles shaking over lives
of young men offered up by their nation,
for renewed struggle with an invisible scar.

He clicks off the war, lost
to memories of duty purchased with human lives.
Absently, the fingers of a nation find his scar.

*Rick King is a SCADA Technician who lives in Valdez, Alaska,
where the sunless winters are ideal for personal reflection and
intense writing.*

MUTE FORCE

When they dropped the A-bombs
on Japan, I was too little
to do anything about it
and had to believe what the grown-ups said
about them deserving it,
us the good guys safe and sound
in our living room watching the newsreel
on my father's home movie projector,
Tommy Dorsey's "Boogie Woogie"
playing on the record player
my father's irony, that '78 for
background music his sense of fair play
as the mushroom clouds boomed silently
shattering the eardrums, tongues, bones,
and souls of all those invisible,
deserving human beings
as images of teen aged jitterbuggers
filled our minds

bombclouds and boogiers forever binding in mine

even now
as I sit watching the bad news on tv
that they've bombed Baghdad
the tv sound off as
Peter Jennings, Bush, and stern
grown-up men from Paris, London,
Washington, and Jerusalem move
their hands and mouths wordlessly,
squint and blink their eyes into the tv lights
and explain, report soundlessly
about the bombs and The War,

men with bald heads, or goatees, white beards,
men with neither tongues nor speech
because I can't bear to turn on the tv sound
and listen to the screech-bombing
and shriek-boogying
because I'm still too little
to do anything about it.

Joan Jobe Smith lives in Long Beach, California, with her husband. She is the founding editor of the literary journal, "Pearl."

THE WAR AGAINST RAPE

when President Bush announced
the United States government
would not tolerate rape . . .

> *I saw women parking in ramps without mace*
> *I saw girls strolling unguarded in parks*
> *I saw co-eds safely asleep in dorm rooms*
> *I saw doors without dead bolt locks*
> *I saw windows open on hot summer nights*
> *I saw children without any scars*
> *I saw women without wounds*

. . . of Kuwait by Iraq.

> *I saw freedom*

The president reported that during the invasion
as many as seven thousand might have been killed.
He said it was our moral duty to kill (Iraqi women
and children, collaterally speaking) to restore
the Emir to his country where women can't vote.

> *held in reserve*

A woman/girl is raped every 60 seconds in the U.S.
1,440 a day; 10,080 every week; 525,600 each year.
How many of them are killed or injured permanently
(collaterally, speaking) in this *Land of the Free.*

> *for those who oil*

Thirty thousand fled from Kuwait to Saudi Arabia.
Only seven thousand Kuwaiti men joined the army.
The Kuwaiti men, it seems, prefer disco clubs.
5% of the U.S. forces in Saudi Arabia were women.

the war machine.

Mary R. DeMaine is an Art History teacher and an archaeologist who has visited and worked at sites around the world. She also skiis and plays the piano for fun.

JANUARY 17, 1991

The day after war begins I
reach to hold, be held
beneath the crescent sliver of waxing snow moon
I feel your chest press   retreat   as we embrace
silken hair weaves through finger-
tips.   Men and women die
in a city no longer theirs no longer
home. Your arms wrap me
as water holds wreaths
and Iraq retaliates
missiles strike Jerusalem
a ten year old girl cries within the brown
mantis face of her gas mask.
Pressed peach of our cheeks
parts my lips near the tenderness of your neck—
I want to feel
your breath on my tongue
your tongue as I breathe.
And what of those in Baghdad
no warning?

*Elizabeth Oakley is a student at San Francisco State University.
She works at the Poetry Center, the Haight Ashbury Free Medical
Center, and provides massages.*

MARKETPLACE REPORT
JANUARY 23, 1991

The new war is a week old.
Bombs fall on Baghdad,
missiles on Tel Aviv.
The man on the radio says
the armament dealers of Europe
are hopeful that a longer war
will be good for business.
They say, as fighting continues
there will be wear and tear
on matériel. Spare parts
must be manufactured,
as well as replacements
for equipment blown apart,
shattered, set afire.

Prudently, the merchants
consult their spreadsheets.
They guard against euphoria
and prepare for a possible
downside to this bonanza:
the Allies are shooting
at their best customer,
Saddam Hussein. If he loses
their market will be depressed.
There is also a danger of
restrictions on sales
to tinpot dictators. Thus,
the long term effects of the war
may not all be positive.

Julie Alger has moved from California to Amherst, Massachusetts. She has worked as a school librarian, a store manager, a proofreader.

SEEN ON THE EVENING NEWS. JANUARY 24, 1991

A Desert Thanatopsis

Somewhere in Arabia see the silhouettes
darkly against the evening sky.
Two U.S. G.I.'s are digging in.

One, the pick man, full-arc swings and
splits the rock-strewn ground.
The other thrusts his shovel in. It clinks on
rock and bites the Arabian soil. He tosses
bite after bite up and out as the two men,
together, form their dugout.

But could it be, instead, their grave? Should they trust
this hole where gas heavy with death may sink
one night, before they can pull on their surreal masks?

Or will the shifting desert soil
defeat the dugout's buttressing,
take back the space the shoveler has claimed,
crushing and smothering the buddies?

High above, the gods of technological war
contend in the ultimate century-end rumble.
With a thump   Scud   whoosh   flash,
manufactured meteors shoot and collide.
Yet, in this fractured sky, no men die,

while the pick-and-shovel soldiers in their
desert hiding-hole silently join the
innumerable caravan that moves below.

144

Then what Scheherazade will tell their tale—of how
two fighting men with pick and shovel dug a hole,
braced its walls, wrapped their Army blankets about them
and
lay down to dream their dreams, then died
before they got to fire a shot?

Jessie Moinuddin, Professor of Biochemistry and Nutrition in the Division of Basic Medical Sciences at Mercer University School of Medicine, has retired from paid teaching to the volunteer faculty.

AT WAR IN THE CATAMOUNT RANGE

We sit around a wood stove
and speak of peace in these days of
high-tech war. We mend moth holes
and wind black yarn to the size of
a cannon ball. We sip tea, smell
chocolate cookies baking.
The noon count was 5000 sorties.
Sortir means to leave and
I wish we would.
We name our small decisions:
to stand in zero weather at
Westover listening to hawks
scream obscenities and wave
"Kick Ass" banners; to write
letters to Washington in the
midst of nursing and diapering;
to take in an extra child and
hide her father in these woods
if he chooses not to fight;
to listen to the sober talk of husbands and sons, and the
anger
and dismay of little boys.
Is the war far from here, Mommy?
What about the kids where
the bombs are dropping?
Do their mommies and daddies
keep them safe?

*Maureen Kennedy teaches music and runs the Senior Companion
Program at the County Mental Health Association in Greenfield,
Massachusetts.*

GOOD MORNING AMERICA

Folks wake up in L.A. to
Good Morning America, in Salt Lake City
and Omaha, the same. News of the war
choreographed between recipes for ribs
and the latest Hollywood scoop.
Wake up to plastic flags in the boulevard,
yellow ribbons, five for a dollar.
"God, Guns and Guts made America free."
It says so, right there on the bumper
of the big car at the red light.

In the desert, morning crawls out early
along with the heat. Soldiers tell themselves
again why they are there. Gather up
their version of the world, put one foot
in front of the other. Soldiers on both sides
watch the dawn sky, looking for stubborn stars,
for their parents' eyes, for any light at all.

The dead travel home in bags and boxes.
When they arrive, children stare
and imagine the body still breathing.
Adults buy flowers, talk silk and oak,
try to walk next to themselves
for an arm to lean on.

*Kathleen Patrick is a poet and writer of fiction. She lives and
writes in St. Louis Park, Minnesota with her husband and her
two young children.*

WHILE HUSSEIN KNEELS ON A PRAYER RUG

and Bush goes to church
with Billy Graham
we are dropping bombs
around the clock
and Hussein vows to fight
until "the last child."
We pat ourselves on our backs
that we are not precisely
aiming for humans
but buildings.
And Hussein did not mean his
own children, for heaven's sake.

Lest you forget,
this is not a war for oil.
We're killing these people to . . .
. . . to save them?

I CAN'T FORGET WHAT HUSSEIN SAID,

"The mother of all wars has begun."
And I hear in the other ear
Bush saying, "This will not be
another Vietnam,"
but already
we are keeping death score
not in bodies this time
but planes
and always, yes, we have downed
at least one more of theirs
than they have of ours.
And already
we are perpetually winning
with no end in sight.
And already
we are manufacturing
reasons to be proud,
putting a face on slaughter
as truthful as make-up
on a corpse.

Belinda Subraman is an editor for "Vergin Press" which pub-lishes works to raise social consciousness. She spent many years in Europe and now lives in El Paso, Texas.

BUDDY LEE PERRIMAN REFLECTS ON THE PERSIAN GULF CRISIS, DAY 15

Some redheaded woman from Kentucky and her two kids
and black dog
Drove up in a brand new jap twodoor
And moved into the old yellow woodframe cross the alley

That was Tuesday then Zettie's stepson Herschell got
pissdrunk
And plowed his damn Harley into a fencepost on 52 the day
after

I had to hock that gook k-bar I got at Vung Tau to raise his
bail
When I come back I seen Riley Frazier the roofer got laid off
Come out of Ike's Recovery Room headed down the unem-
ployment office

Then this morning one of them young kids from cross the
way come over
A little skinny boy with peanut butter and jelly stains on his
chin
Dirty blue jeans tore out at both knees and his hair not
washed proper you could tell

Mister, he says, they got a new war on TV and my momma
she gonna buy me and my sister Goddam Saddam t-shirts
and a scud video game
Soon as our ADC check come in

Hey mister, he says
Was you born in that wheelchair?

Son, I says, set down on that box of empties right there and
I'll tell you a story
About three bears lived in a jungle
Mama-san, Papa-san and Baby-san . . .

*L.E. McCullough has worked as a book publisher, musician,
college teacher, radio announcer, journalist, and advertising
copywriter. He lives in Minneapolis.*

A PLEA TO THE SCRIBNER OF ORMUZ
(Persian Gulf, February 1991)

Scribner of Ormuz,
Your calligraphy of bent
Foam rinsed in oily rain,

Inscribe a lamentation for the children
Who cannot topple the towers of pitchsmoke
Nor hush their billowing roar.

Inscribe the sun seeping through
A wadding of stained clouds to weave
A dark cocoon in the souring heat.

Inscribe tidal flats measled with slick
And cormorants who sit bewildered,
Hobbled with clotted wings.

Inscribe Kurdish tears in the spume of the sea.

Inscribe their ragtag procession
Like torn butterflies clinging to ledges
While tiny fists of rain crumple their faces.

Inscribe a swelling of untreated wounds,
A bog of daunted eyes, a sob of borders.

Inscribe a lamentation for the wide blue dome
Whose soot of grief glazes the minaret
In the once fragrant garden of Simran.

Scribner of Ormuz,
Release the light that crouches in black rain
That we may find some place to wash and receive our dead.

Frances Stillman-Linderman hitchhiked through Morocco, France, Greece, Turkey, Syria, Iraq, Iran, Pakistan and India in 1963-64. She formed a deep affection for that part of the world.

IN THE VALLEY OF THE SHADOW OF

Again the old men found us an enemy,
the afterimage of the last one still flickering
behind our eyelids. Before we could climb weary
from our bunkers, blinking moistly in
the unaccustomed glare. While even those most clever
with their hands fumbled at the puzzle
of beating plowshares out of swords. All we like sheep
tied on yellow ribbons and cheered.

Our old women saw visions, our young women
dreamed dreams. Prophesied conflagration,
our anointed heads of state
bombing Eden back before creation
for a jug of oil. They dreamed volleys of blue fire,
lethal arcs of light across a night sky,
small children donning elephant masks
against the airborne plagues to come.

On the screen grey men in suits spoke earnestly
with other men, splitting hairs
with pocket knives. Counting down
deadlines, numbering legions, with obvious
arousal they described the implements of battle.
Patriarchs and politicians intoned necessity
and righteousness, dared distant adversaries
to cross lines drawn with sticks in the sand.

Outside a library, a young man beat a dark-haired woman,
a stranger, because
she wore Arabic letters on her shirt.
An angry man cutting yellow ribbons from doorways
was locked in an asylum. In Babylon,
a small wounded boy lies on a stretcher, his round eyes
half his face with fear. He tugs at his tattered clothes
with modesty, to cover himself, and looks up
direct and unblinking at us until hoisted away.

Darby Penney is a planner for the New York State Office of Mental Health. She also edits the "Snail's Pace Review" in Cambridge, New York.

EVERYONE SAID

"If it were done
then 'twere well it were done quickly."
Right?
That's what everyone said.
We gotta go in, do the job
and get out fast
I did notice that people who said
we gotta go
weren't going anywhere.
They meant other people's
children had to go

As wars go
this was a wonderful war
as wars go
Iraqui mothers saw their children
incinerated
That's the cost
Cheap at the price
Wonderful war
So why am I sad?
Cheap at the price
the smart money said
So why am I sad?
If I'm sad
how do you suppose
that Iraqui mother feels?

Rita Nolan Giglio has worked in advertising, publishing, teaching and politics. She has raised two daughters in whom she is well pleased.

EMPIRE

The pages already flutter in the wind,
but the boastful Honorius idles at court.
He doesn't feel the cold gusting from the East,
or see the yellow glare staining

the horizon. He waves his hand
and palaces bloom, church walls shimmer
with unearthly colors. In his dreams,
Alaric the Visigoth keeps breaking camp

and his brother Ataulfus drinks toasts
from a skull. Within the gates,
commerce as usual, the rulers amuse themselves
by watching bears maul prisoners.

As the pages fall like leaves from the weakened
spine, we seed the clouds, unleashing
electronic storms. The president proclaims
that our banners will snap in the wind,

though in his dreams, barbarians
seep through our cities. Behind the walls,
we hang on while the century
darkens and a bear-claw of hunger

tightens its grip. It was only yesterday,
that our hot-blooded leader mimicked
Honaria, the empress's daughter
who sent a ring and a letter to Attila the Hun.

*Marguerite Bouvard is a political scientist and poet who is a
visiting research scholar at the Wellesley College Center for
Research on Women, and author of several books.*

YELLOW RIBBONS

I am so sick
Of seeing yellow ribbons
Tied to antennas
Flapping dirty on the freeway
Flags dripping loose
In the flat suburbs
Or stickered plastic
On the windows of
Neighborhood stores

Sometimes I think
There may be enough
To decorate the corpses
Rotting
Dismembered
In the scalding sun of the Middle East

Elaine Beale, originally from England, says she was as horrified by England's response to the war as she was by that of the United States.

DISTANCES

These yellow ribbons festoon the gift of war
opened so eagerly, the promise that some new
appliance will whir us into ease and happiness.

We are a people of gadgets, in love
with mechanisms that can intercede
between our hands and the task to be done.

Better to rip those pilots out of the air,
equip them with knives and etch in their minds
crosshairs that target organs and arteries.

Better that they should find the skin
of their victims under their nails, and for days
pluck dark strands of hair from their uniforms.

Mary Makofski has worked as a health instructor for Planned Parenthood and is now an English Instructor at Orange County Community College in Middletown, New York.

DRIVE-BY PATRIOTISM

Flags wave
Yellow ribbons flutter from
their staffs
Some droop
in the Southern California heat
or snap ragged
from car antennas
drive-by patriotisnm
the blue and the red and the white
a blanket to shelter ourselves
a beacon to guide the way
a blindfold to hid our eyes

Alina Tugend is the environmental reporter for the Orange County Register in California. She is 31 and lives with her husband, Mark, in Long Beach.

MAYDAY!

Ribbons tied to Fourth Avenue trees
dangle, unnoticed,
frost-starched brightness
laundered all spring
to a nameless gray,

remnants of an urge to demonstrate
a sentiment on which not all agreed.
Some mistook their boastfulness for reason.
A heady feeling let them wave the flag,
gulled them to accept that war was justified.

Our lives seem better since the news
no longer harps on scuds and carpet bombing.
The horror shows we watched have yet
to film their final episodes.
Help us if this is only intermission.

Hundred thousand dreams exploded.
How many might that be?
A human brain cannot absorb
a shock of such dimension.
Whose children make up such a number?

Those thousands, could we have
that many enemies?
We think ourselves a friendly people.
Why do we limit grief,
compassion to our own?

We must now wait
for the conclusion,
learn what force we have set free,
what price will be exacted
when all accounts are drawn.

Some night a workman on the avenue
will mount his ladder to unbind
those bows and tatters,
tokens of a war,
ribbons that were their own parade.

May 1, 1991

Winifred Jaeger, born in Brooklyn, New York, grew up in World War II Berlin. She now combines teaching recorder and piano with a career as legal assistant in Seattle.

AFTERMATH

When Desert Shield became a Storm,
I couldn't bring myself to buy a flag.
I prayed for peace,
bought a yellow ribbon for my door.

I joined the dwindling ranks of doves,
retreated into silence,
while hawks, the owners of the sky,
ranged free.

Forgotten in the aftermath of victory:
the San Francisco march, the signs
that read, *Deplorable*
and *18 males per gallon.*

Amid the waving flags
and welcome home parades,
faces of the dead and maimed recede.
Let's revel and forget
that there is something still out there
that wants to kill.

Linda Ashear runs writing workshops for people from second grade to senior citizens. She lives and writes in Irvington, New York.

SHAME

March 1991
> "And yellow was the multiplying sand . . ."
> Dylan Thomas

1.

Now in the pre-ornamental spring
ice-covered ruts thaw underfoot
and puddles open up like eyes. What
does the water see before it disappears
to make it fall on us again like rain?

2.

It is the wrong season.
It's X-mas we want. And snow.
Snow to block windows, to freeze
shut the eyes of water. Snow
in high drifts packed snug against
the house. Not flurries but storms,
snows of ribbons, blizzards of ribbons,
one hundred and fifty thousand sleet-
blinding yellow ribbons to decorate
the axed trees of bone, to camouflage
the stiff packages of flesh, to cover
the coffins that insist on being counted,
crawling up out of the sand.

How many miles of the stuff
can we manufacture? How much taffeta?
Grosgrain? Curl-with-a scissor acetate?
How many bobbins? It will take
nine yards to wrap around each box—
each gift of grief—plus
the two feet necessary for a bow

and we'll need plenty left for lapels,
corsages, wreaths, plenty to sell Boy Scouts
and beer, to wrap trees and a streak
of yellow over our eyes.

3.

We have added death to death
and call it a clean new arithmetic,
with no word for subtraction.

A general is our new sex symbol.
He holds up his pants with ribbons.
He loops up his fly with ribbons.
He wishes codpieces were fashionable.

Even God is decorated: his skull
lacing yellow in and out
the sockets of his eyes: God
of maggot and the shame of angels
waving his yellow banner
in front of his television—
rooting for the home team.

4.

In the desert
the sweet yellow ribbons
of the body's fat are melting
—yellow, yellow is the multiplying sand.

We have broken decency on the wheel
and are teaching the children to flutter
their little flags in the endless procession.

Alice Friman is a professor of English and Creative Writing at the
University of Indianapolis.

AGING AND DESERT STORM: A DUET

How many Iraqi babies will live to be old?
Why is the soft sorrow of children a faint echo to old men?
How does one grow old and remain innocent?
Why not limit soldiering to age 60 and over?

How many stiffs in the sand eaten by dogs?
Why don't we know the number of dead?
How was it like shooting fish in a barrel?
Why will the old pilot return to visit decades later?

How can the "Butcher of Baghdad" wink at us as we
grumble?
Why weren't smart bombs wrapped in yellow ribbon?
How does the shadow of despair lengthen with age?
Why do our grand intentions wear out before our lives?

How do mothers wrapped in mourning black endure?
How can one hear a human voice in the metal air?

*David Zeiger helped organize anti-Vietnam demonstrations at the
Fashion Institute of Technology where he teaches English. He
also added his support in a vigil against Desert Storm.*

DECEPTION

The toys of war
with cowboy-Indian names
Desert Shield   Desert Storm,
Tomahawks, Apaches and Marauders
play out their deadly games
in far off heat and sand.

The press, obedient, paints
this unholy mess as clean
and bloodless   a superior
production we're expected
to applaud. Behind the curtain
children blow apart
lie dead in heaps of rubble
while on the air
the oily glut of news
clogs my ears and cells.

Here at home
blue shadows stretch
on white untrampeled lawns.
Only a distant crow
and the little squeak of boots
on snow disturb
this winter stillness.

I walk these tranquil streets
where flags and yellow ribbons
decorate the doorways,
stand for a moment
to watch a flight of geese,
the sinking western sun,
wings glued to my sides
a hostage to this war.

Jeanne Shepard, retired, is finally free to enjoy the pleasures and pains of writing after years of marriage, child rearing, work, and study.

FABRIC OF HISTORY

Oh Betsy if you could see it now—
     the oriflamme born in your soft hands
     proudly flown for centuries now
Hung in victory
     while the souls of innocents hang
     between worlds
     in spirit limbo   confused
     by the language of their own deaths:
"Collateral damage" can stop a heart from beating?

Betsy your fine flag now hangs alongside
     countless yellow bows tied by hypnotized
     People-magazine readers
     who believe   who believe   who believe   every-
thing
     CBS and Chevron and Chevrolet say
     is true.

Betsy those yellow ribbons
     celebrating mass murder
     masquerading as peace wishes
     flutter close
     by the freedom sign your gentle hands cut and
     stitched in the night.

Betsy it's right that you were proud.
What ordinary woman ever knows
     how her heart's expression might
     someday be paraded
     or even stained to disguise truth
     and fabricate history?

Geneen Marie Hakala has never before submitted a poem for publication. She could not resist striking a blow against the "fiasco in the Persian Gulf."

SOUND BITES FROM THE BROADCASTS WE NEVER TUNED IN

If the cries of
torn and burning victims
could travel thousands of miles,
would the football metaphors
describing the exuberant infliction of pain
and the cheerleading stop?

If the screams of
broken children
and their shattered mothers
moaned from the walls
of every comfortable corporate office
and agony reverberated audibly
through all American subdivisions,
would the average person
finally comprehend the actual meaning
of collateral cost?

From pulpits, the new military messiahs
invoke holy nintendo spirits,
clean neutron killing fields,
raise red hands to salute
a fascist god.

The congregation suffers testosterone poisoning,
chants for more ground-action entertainment,
more belligerent death,
and their voices are loud.

The bomb-battered aliens
writhe silently just beyond microphone range
within the ragged craters of Patriot tombs.

Recent American Wars

America's ears are filled
with an endless loop
of nationalistic white noise,
the whimpers of civilian casualties
turned too low for any carrying sound.

2/17/91

*Jennifer Lagien is a technical writer for a library automation
vender. She is also an active leader and worker with several
peace organizations.*

WARBALL

The Superbowl of History
Is playing in the desert
Brimming with dead boys.
What's another deadboy
To add into the mixture?
They go down easy.

The superbowl of History
Is a cauldron
As empty and big as
A lion's mouth.

The Superbowl of History
Bubbles in the sandstorm.
The dunes resound with hyperbole
And give off the fragrance of deceit.

The desert sun flares
As the cauldron simmers.
The stew is never finished,
And the game goes on.

*Esther Crystal teaches Creative Writing at Touro College and is
the daughter of a Holocaust survivor which she believes strength-
ens her anti-war position.*

THE EYES OF HAGAR'S CHILDREN

The eyes of Hagar's children,
Enormous, dark and beautiful,
Reproach us with the hurt therein revealed.
What is the nature of the child's offence?

When Ishmael lay exposed
And near to death in arid wilderness,
When Hagar lifted her voice
And cried her bitter tears,
An angel came to her.

Are Hagar's promised progeny
Less worthy of God's love?
Are we to be forgiven for inflicting pain
Because we call the hurt *collateral?*
Large, dark and beautiful, pure Iraqi eyes,
Plead earnestly for justice, as bombs fall from the skies.

*Raymond F. Rogers has had a number of his poems published
since he retired from the Postal Service.*

MINE EYES HAVE SEEN

Clean win, State-of-the Art weapons and video
games selected, projected with gleeful exultation.
Glory Hallelujah. Blackout, trash swept underneath
the sand, but limbs peek out; still, no death in sight.
A turkey-shoot: bullets aimed at running backs punctured,
gape like tulips spattering their color.

Glory Glory Hallelujah.

Three pairs of eyes, salt draining onto bearded cheeks,
inhale the limp crinkled doll-like figure next to open plot
of sandy earth, two by three. A stained white cloth is
folded,
hugs the body, gently   gently lowered. Then the dirt is
scooped
into the hole, gulping it until there is no sign.

Eighty-eight thousand tons of Hi-Tech massacred the flee-
ing,
wiped off a father's nose, his chin while winds of death
spread
poison into wailing souls. The chinless Kurd-man says: we
thought your president would chop Hussein's head off,
instead
pulled out, left us nailed to the cross.

Glory Glory Hallelujah.

Outside, red   white   blue   yellow ribbon party-time: we're
#1 and
don't forget it. Inside, we're not so sure. Inside, we
watched our country swallow up another, then regurgitate.
What are we
celebrating. Tiny shriveled faces. Oil wells. Liquid sewage.

Our truth is marching on.

*J.B. Bernstein works full-time at the Regional Water Authority
and is active in Women's Issues.*

THE CRADLE OF CIVILIZATION

Where the Tigris and Euphrates meet,
human beings planted seeds and stayed
long enough to harvest them,
stayed again,
created settlements, and towns,
surplus, art, philosophy and written laws,
a stable body politic on common ground.
This is where the world we know began.

How very far we've come
that we should come to such a place
not with gratitude and wonder
but with bombs and guns,
that we should not find this odd,
that we should so believe our otherness
that we would rather kill and die
than search for common ground.

W.E. Ehrhart is a Marine Corps Veteran of Vietnam. He lives in Philadelphia, Pennsylvania, with his wife and daughter.

THE BIRDS OF PREY

ancient image
in Rome before
a war augurers neatly
dissected birds
and read their entrails
seeking guidance
this practise
I once thought
barbaric

late news image
one soldier teaches another the art
of desert survival
holding a beautiful
white bird
he sinks his teeth into
its softly breathing chest
and eats it alive

irretrievable image
the dove leaves the ark
finds the green
plucks the promise

late breaking image
oil black bird
spreads its wings on
the sand
waits to die

broken image
the holy spirit
ascending
transcending
turns suddenly
plummets towards earth

forsaken image
the cries of birds
lure us back
towards sanctity
and the meaning returns
to the sacrifice
pure
white
and undevoured.

Gail Golden is a psychotherapist with special interest in feminism and issues of creativity.

BLOOD FOR OIL

Must the crimson blood of humankind
be spilled so machines may drink
the black blood of dinosaurs?
Must we offer the lives
of our husbands, wives or children
to feed the insatiable thirst
of trains, planes and automobiles
that pollute our air, water and land
with their excremental slime?
Must we preserve fat bellied oil companies
who in the midst of crisis ask us
to slice our economic wrists,
then gouge us for the privilege
of defending their interests?
Must we act the role
of the world's policemen
when we barely tolerate our own?
Must we act on behalf of those countries
who refuse to act for themselves?
Will those who benefit from our sacrifice
pay us back for our grievous losses—
can they give life to the dead?

William Scott Galasso is committed to "life on this planet." He works with environmental groups, Amnesty International, Habitat for Humanity, and others.

PARAPHRASING THE GULF WAR

Our government in Washington's intent
to talk of war in language that is bent,
citing bombing raids as "air sorties"
as if it is discussing angered bees.
It's eighteen thousand tons of TNT
in ten hours drop on foreign entity.

The General in charge mouthes softly "KIAs",
men blown to bits in one twelve-hour phase.
Defense man labels Scud missiles "old-fashioned"
and "weapons of terror", Iraq's innacurate passion.
"Precise and surgical devices" named "Cruise"
and "Patriot" are deadlier than what Iraqis use.

Biological weapons we brand inhumane,
but crippling Baghdad's water system is sane.
And what if typhus epidemics break out?
"Unintended collateral damage" we'll shout.

We say it's a test between evil and good.
Do we always do what we properly should?
"Liberation of Kuwait" has a lofty sound.
It means restoring monarchy to former ground.

In this war, words used, soften actualities
and phrases indirect, mask realities.

*Ella Cavis has retired from teaching English to Bradenton,
Florida.*

A CONCISE HISTORY OF THE OIL WAR

The King of Kuwait,
An unsavory state,
Got attacked by another dictator
with absolute powers
(But not one of ours,
So that made him a ruthless invader).

He was Saddam Hussein,
and he'd already slain
His own citizens, hand over fist.
So the U.N. forces
Rode up on white horses
And slaughtered the ones that he missed.

Now, our quarrel was not
With the folks that we shot,
We just thought it would make them rebel,
But instead, they were dead,
And the last words they said
Were, "Yankee, go home or to hell!"

And so, now, at least
There's peace in the East,
Since there's nobody left in Iraq
Excepting Hussein,
Softly racking his brain
For a nuclear plan of attack.

He can hardly succeed.
The components he'd need
Are controlled by American dealers.
Still, they *could* use the dough,
And it's too soon to know,
But I hear they've been putting out feelers.

David Gladish does cement work for six months of the year so he can write for the other six.

FATHERS' NIGHT

The President paints black on the sky
Schoolboys draw war machines.
Teacher buys the paper,
no money for books.
Girl writes, "Who is the winner?"
Rivers, seas polluted, thousands of babies dead,
first human art dust.
Meditator breathes in dark.
"Why prefer death?" the Goddess asks.

Where did your job,
where did your money,
schools, democracy, free speech go?
Where did your breast, your fetus, your sleep go?
Once there was kissing in the streets.
Where did the trees go?
Where did your mind go?

Insomnia, anxiety, depression, infertility,
chronic pain, incessant weeping, uncontrollable panic,
heart-break in every relationship
are signs of empire's fall.
Survival, knowledge, happiness—
the feeling we are loved—
are all that humans want.
But no one can be happy
living in an evil empire.

Trees rustle, "Dying
in this air."
Mountains moan, "Looting and stripping—
we have no snow."
Men shout, "We need more."
"Heart flees,"the poet writes.
Teacher says, "You must change your mind."

Easy to say no
to war, violence, greed,
confusion, emptiness,
cruel brute strength.
You have eyes that brighten,
hands that soften,
souls that knows justice.
You are alive,
can value your own life.

Kogis open the Mountain Gate:
"Younger Brother has robbed the Mother,
She who is fertility and intelligence,
whose blood is gold.
Does Younger Brother see?
The world does not have to end
but it will end, unless he understands."

Black, on black, on black—
not a street light, not a flash light,
only a candle. Dissolved in dark,
Her body is the one you love,
abundant and flowering, fragrant and warm
as it grows darker, and darker, and darker,
and you dive in Her dark,
you die in Her dark,
disappear in the darkness inside Her.

Janine Canan is a psychiatrist who writes and travels extensively.

THE RULES

This time the bodybags will be called
"pouches"
and the war, "a use of force."
Murder will be known as
"collateral damage"
and missiles—"Patriots."
And if by tomorrow
Hussein is a "Hitler"
we can justify every last act
and each carpet-bombed "A-rab" village
we will brag has been
"liberated."

I *Susan Erem is a union organizer in the Chicago area.*

INDIFFERENCE

the neon lights of cities
flare over ocean and shore
raping the purity of distance
on seas' surface the sly cunning
of oil-slick murders defenseless life:
at the heart of the world, gibbets swing
gorged, slow and stupefied with death
cries of earth's beggars resound
within the vault of man's uncaring

maddened by folly and waste
tormented by indifference
my fury and despair are hurled
into the dissolving wind:

there is no answer
only the ache of doleful echoes
hesitating on desecrated air
and perception of earth's beauty
broken, lost, impossible to regain
a sense of balance gone awry
a prescience of desolate waters
homeless birds, unchanging winter

covering a white planet.

Hannah Alexander has written scripts for Hollywood movies and served as translator for French and German films.

SHADES OF TRUTH

Sun glances off
shades of red
as they bleed
into the desert.
God is in our cock-
pit, force is born
from the Latin "fortis"
"I am stronger
than you are." Thumb in nose.
"You will do what I say." Boom.
Resort to bombs
in the name
of law and order. Boom
and then noiseless houses
with shades drawn,
empty streets, dead
cold light of tomorrow:
time is orphan
in this age
of hype and hallucination,
as ruby lights play
across sand.
That child in the ditch
is only an average tragedy
in this epoch of tears,
spilt over roseate altar rails,
over bars, glove-muffled sobs,
earthquake shudders that rock cities,
prime pumps, fill lakes, great ocean-
wave of tears,
streaked, blurred magentas—
greens—yellows
of houses merge with trees—
lawns—streets, dun sky
where cars are always departing.
Weep sagas, eulogies, epics.
Rubicund language of loss.
It is in the darkness of his eyes,

that a man is lost. After he sees
a child's face explode
how is sleep ever possible again?
What if there were only lips
left to scream?
Imagine all that red: Inflamed desert,
claret sea, sanguine storm.
The first casualty
of war is truth.
Every missile
sends ripples through
the universe. No more leaves
stand clear and separate.
Twigs quiver with fear.
Deep within he feels
his world ending,
with a headline, a slogan,
a fiction redder than the Cedars
of Lebanon. Pax Americana.
Fang baring. Brilliant display
of plumage.

I *Constance Studer is a registered nurse, now retired.*

REMARKS ON THE GULF WAR

Why must we give this man,
who rejoices only in destruction,
so much joy?

—   —   —

On this dark plain,
sad am who sane.

—   —   —

"The spiral of history . . ."— —
like down the drain

—   —   —

"Nothing is worth dying for."
That's right, we do it for nothing.

—   —   —

Our bigotry is embedded in language:
We must learn to call them, not "evil"
or "psychotic", but rather "morally
challenged" and "ethically impaired."

—   —   —

War on Iraq— —
Serves 'em right, using a "q"
without a "u"!

—   —   —

  The Medium is the Mess

Next war, we won't have to put up
with repetitive news "flashes" and hours of
"background." Those who can afford it
will buy direct satellite links, each
to his or her own assigned soldier,
wired for sight, sound, emotion . . .
The less affluent will be linked to
quartermaster clerks and aides.
We will be able to follow the progress
of the war (from our limited viewpoints)
minute by minute. Greedily we'll exchange
our dope. We'll know the boredom,
the tragedy: "Joe, is it true,

We Speak for Peace

did your number come up last night?"
"Yes . . . yes." "Was it . . . " "I can't
talk about it yet." "Did you stay with it
to the end." "Yes." "Good man."

— — —

*Dean Blehert works for the U.S. government and is a member of
Federal Poets and Publisher of Deannotations.*

BLACK DOVE

Before the war we knew the enemy
We knew his face
But when it began
The war became the enemy
And its face was every face:

It was the waiting of the worried mother;
It was the face of fear
The young man wore as a new uniform;
It was the wrench of wild eyes
Looking for food;
It was the stupor of eyes
looking for sleep;
It was the child whose eyes were burned,
And she could no longer cry;
It was the face of a thousand children
Who could do nothing but cry;
It was the man who came back
Without a face
And his is the face we remember
When we remember the war.

And when peace came
We were told
That it was a ream of fine paper
Blotting the black ink
Of so many black scrawls
Of so many men who did this.

And the radio gave the report
And sang us a song:
> *See this treat peace*
> A dove released
> Look to the skies
> *See the dove rise*
But we could not see it
Because the skies were black
And so was the dove.

Shulamith Bat-Yisreal is a native of Texas.

MEDITATION ON THE GULF WAR

L1:   Truly the light is sweet and a pleasant thing it is to behold the sun. A fallen soldier's loss is multiplied; the young sweetness dies in his eyes, and ever after we hear the victor, the broken King crying, Absalom, Absalom, my son."

P.   JERUSALEM WAS CARVED OUT OF DAVID'S HEART. THE SOUL OF THE HOLY CITY BECAME AN UNDEFENDED FORT. WE ARE ALL FATHERS AND MOTHERS, SONS AND DAUGHTERS, AND WE HAVE BUT A LITTLE WHILE TOGETHER.

L2:   Then we heard that God had ordained peace: it shall run like a river and our sons and daughters shall study war no more.

P.   BUT WE CRAVE POWER. WE ARE THE ONLY ANIMAL WITH A PENCHANT FOR REARRANGING THE MAP OR FOR SAVAGING OUR OWN KIND.

All: Yet we have another dispensation: to build the community of shalom, to gather cosmos out of chaos, to take them in whom we have injured.

L3.   Refugees from our policies toward Central America keep streaming northward to accept us, saying "thy people shall be my people and thy ways my ways."

L1.   We crave power: we live in another terror where untold wealth is deployed to protect our remaining riches by destroying the earth.

P.   MOTHER, PRAY FOR US, AND FOR THE EARTH. IT WEARS YOUR BLUE MANTLE IN SWIRLS, I CATCH SIGHT OF YOU WITH THE CHILD HERE AND THERE. IT'S ALL RIGHT, THEN, YOU'VE MADE IT ONCE MORE.

L2 and L3:

       Lady, protectress, come visit, gently my nightmares where the nuclear bombs I've paid for are aimed at my child and me. How did you wrap your child for the flight into Egypt?

L1:   I'm using wet sheets, but, Mother! he saw the fire-ball and has no eyes to see.

P.   DELIVER US FROM COVETING GOD'S POWER.

L2:   I saw you, Mother, in Baghdad, on the news. You were little and brown, and you had a son, in the war. Your mosque had been bombed so you turned, resolute, to a church. You lit a taper and proffered it urgently to the mother of the Son.

L3.   Everything that rises must converge. But in the next few days from safe in the sky we killed a hundred thousand sons in what we called the ground war.

P.   LORD HAVE MERCY UPON US, AND ON THEM. THEIR LEADER HAS COMMITTED NAKED AGRESSION AND UNSPEAKABLE ATROCITIES AND HELD A WHOLE COUNTRY CAPTIVE, AND MUCH OIL. THESE THINGS COULD NOT STAND. WE DID THAT PART WITHOUT PRESS COVERAGE.

L1:   And yet thy voice came: the blood of thy brothers and sisters cry to me from the ground.

P.   LORD, LORD, IT WAS US.

L2:   May the 100,000 dead Iraqis rest in the boson of Ali, as it is written. May the 89 dead Anmericans be too many for another war.

L3.   And as if that were not enough, we said to a weak subject people in a stage whisper, go kill the tyrant for us— we'll back you up—and you will be free. When they rose up like the children of Israel . . . We must have known what would happen, we must have known about pogroms, but our press couldn't face it again. It waited for a better subject for our living rooms and gave us the sequel, the exodus, and spared us most of the dying and all the raping, the pulling beards off the men, napalming civilians from gunships and finishing up with machine guns. One baby, dead of exposure is a human interest story; one, dying because its mother lived through too much terror to be able to let down her milk.

P.   GOD, MAKE US HASTEN TO THE TIME WHEN THE REMNANT OF THE KURDISH PEOPLE SHALL SIT EVERYONE UNDER THEIR OWN VINE AND FIG TREE AND NONE MAY MAKE THEM AFRAID.

L, L2, L3:   For all those, on all sides, who have been in authority, God, have mercy upon them. For all those who have been obedient, have mercy on them. For all those of us who have prayed with too faint a heart,

ALL: Have mercy on us. Now gathered together, we grieve for all the lives cut short—the Iraqui lives, the American lives, the Kuwaitis, the Saudis, the British, the Egyptians, the Israelis, the French . . . and all the parents here and over there, whose lives are broken.

We grieve for the many who have suffered torture at the hands of the Iraqui's and for the Palestinians who have suffered at the hands of the Kuwaitis, and for the Kurdish people, savaged and betrayed and dying destitute, barefoot, over the mountain ice, cradling their dead infants till they find a spot of earth, for burial. And we grieve for the sea, the animals and the air that have been poisoned in this strange war.

L1:   Truly the light is sweet and a pleasant thing it is to behold the sun.

This service was sponsored by the Wellesley, Massachusetts Interfaith Peace Committee.

Barbara Mohr is a German translator and the mother of three, one of whom is an Indian daughter received from Mother Theresa.

SUMMATION

I am not proud.
The air carries summons of victory,
Of body counts and huddled prisoners in the sand,
Bunkers demolished and cities destroyed.
We have entered the midnight lanes of death
Amid the cries of the bereaved and suffering.
I feel cloistered, betrayed,
Unwilling to acknowledge the destruction
My country has wrought.

Warriors wave and jubilant crowds applaud.
Instruments of death have been unleashed
Upon the innocent and the guilty alike.
I have had enough of generals with shiny medals
Dissecting the progress of annihilation.

Ruthlessness is not restricted to foreign lands alone.
It touches the mighty, the powerful, the civilized,
Leaders who control the fragile destiny
Of the free world.

I weep for those who abandoned the road to peace,
Who have scorned negotiation and human conciliation.
Villains can come in expensive business suits
And sit in the seats of the elite.
What have we gained except a sense of fear
That has permeated the Third World?
We have enunciated a new democratic doctrine,
That might makes fright.

Monarchy and despotism have been restored
To the turbulent Middle East,

While billionaire oilmen gloat
Over the victory of the Beast.

Bernard Forer has been active in the peace movement and the labor movement for most of his adult life. He is 85 years old.

V

Soldiers

Toy Soldier

Little toy soldiers with little toy guns,
All formed in rank and file;
Many a battle they fought and won
For the shine of a little boy's smile.

Now the cannon sits tarnished with age,
The soldiers stand frozen in stare,
Awaiting the touch of tiny hands
That loved and placed them there.

But little men grow up, alas
To march in wars of their own,
And the pain they feel and the deaths they die
Toy soldiers have never known.

Little toy soldiers with little toy guns,
Wearing dust on helmet and pack,
How sad your wait will be in vain—
Your Captain won't be back.

C. David Hay is a dentist whose hobby is Native American artifacts.

SOLDIER

His body
had never been
so toned
so slim

his mind
never so tuned
to danger
and to laughter

body and mind
examined daily
by his commander

like a lamb
destined
for slaughter

Iris Litt writes advertising and commercial copy and dabbles in
real estate.

I LOVED MY COUNTRY

Years ago
In France
I loved my country
When I saw the graves of Americans
Like forests
Spread over the fields of Verdun.
I knew then you cannot mock
A soldier's courage
Only war
The use of war.
The French erected a statue to death, *La Morte,*
On another battlefield
And called death the only victor.
In that morbid forest
I sensed death everywhere.
There is nothing on earth like
The fields of graves of fallen soldiers
Green, carefully tended, hushed, mute
They stand reproachfully, peacefully
The agonies frozen in the air around them
The spirits of the men lingering quietly
Unable, quite, to leave
Unable to quite believe it all has happened
Waiting for us to free them.
They ask us to honor them
To mourn them
And to unknot the tortuous bonds that lead to war.
Only this can free them.
They linger on as much for our sakes
As for theirs.

Jennifer McDowell is a music and book publisher. She has taken the road less traveled which has led to adventure and a skinny budget.

PETERS, ROBERT

Mortar fire, a perfect hit
spoke its savage language
found its quivering target;
the heart of a boy
named Robert Peters
from a river town
in Pennsylvania.

He was a boy
who always finished lawn chores
and got the papers on the porches
before playing softball
for the Blue Jays.

He loved a girl
named Mary, though once
when they were thirteen
he stole her trading card
that looked like Bart,
the Springer Spaniel
he had lost and also loved.

Ike was in the background
while Rob was brought up
on home cooking
and heaps of praise for learning
about courage   how to fix your own car
and the value of a dollar;
by people who raised children   but not questions
about what was right and wrong.

He had a perfect earthly sense of
them, one fleeting final picture:
of home, of Bart, of Mary
after a frantic moment's try
to run   escape   get out of there
and this scream   this plea: not now
not now   not now   not now.

I *Judith R. Robinson* is an editor, a writer, and a painter.

DISGRACE

If Juan Rodriguez is alive today
I'd like to tell him
that to step on a mine
your first step into war

is no disgrace.

What will my mother say?
he asked the medics
bending over him
knowing he shouldn't see
what all he'd lost.

What will she think
of her clumsy son?

I'd like to say
I've seen good men take longer,
long enough to call their country
putrefied;

I knew one boy
who ate gunpowder
and died.

I'd like to say
I've seen men cry
and try to swat the bullets
away like bees;

watched one teenager
scared of dying
shoot off both his knees.

I huddled half my year
in mud
and couldn't remember
my mother's face;

believe me
Juan
your friends who stayed
went far beyond disgrace.

David Hall is a veteran of Vietnam, a husband and father, and a salesman of college textbooks.

SOLDIER STEREOTYPES

We're the stereotypes on your movie screen.
The cynical tough guy from Brooklyn, the sergeant
Whose know-how will save the squad.

We cannot begin to explain what we are, yet
We're the kids who yesterday played on your block.
Today we carry the machine gun tripod.

One of us was a driver for the mob, now he's
Stoned on Sterno: one's a scholar, fluent in Arabic;
The platoon sergeant's a small-time gambler who cheats.

We are not the quiet, courageous kid who will do
The right thing; the heroic officer, star of the film,
Who never gets hit—those guys are already killed.

I remember them well—the officer with his gold teeth
Phoning in the situation from the cellar, while the tank
Points its cannon muzzle down at him.

Samuel Exler has been a hospital, office, warehouse, and social worker, a print production manager, an advertising copywriter, and a psychotherapist. Not a joiner, during the Gulf War, he joined the Veterans for Peace.

SOLDIER SONG

Give your soldier a hand, boys
make him feel at home
Give your soldier a hand, boys
make him feel at home

Take him to the station
try to make his day
Give your soldier a hand, boys
send him on his way

Time is getting late, babe
so much to be done
Time is getting late, babe
rub him 'til he's numb

Make him understand, love
a better world ahead
Make him understand
leave nothing left unsaid

Give your soldier a hand, boys
the train is rollin' in
Give your soldier a hand, boys
no more love to spend

If he comes back in a box
plant him on a hill
If he comes back in a box
love him if you will

Give your soldier a hand, boys
give your soldier a hand
Leave his ashes in a box
upon your windowsill

*Gerry Glombecki is a folk singer, song writer, and a
conscientious objector. He organized the first folk festival in
Tucson, Arizona.*

I SHOT HIM WITH MY GUN
for duke

He was just a young man,
      no more than twenty-one,
His future was before him,
      his life had just begun,
I bet he had a family,
      a wife, a home, a son,
I didn't even know him,
      but I shot him with my gun.

They said go do your duty,
      there's a victory to be won,
Do it for your country,
      I did it, now it's done,
In peace there's always courage,
      in killing there is none,
And just because he's different
      I shot him with my gun.

Edwin J. Doughty *is a pacifist who believes poetry can make a difference.*

HOPE CHEST

Standing alone in solitary rows
    all the gleaming dead soldiers;
marched out under umbrella of
    chivalry and "doing the right thing."

They are young boys, not weaned from
    soda pop; young girls, who,
still are collecting the innocent hope
    for those lacy virginal chests.

These vessels of hope and deliverance
    are foolishly pitted against the
insanity of the persian slipper; who, is
    armed, with inflated ego and fiery bloodlust.

These lofty ideals become shrouds of
    humanitarianism; that, are truths bedecked
in horsehair suits and worn by the youths
    into war unto death.

Return the battle to a board game and let
    the lads graduate to hardier ales;
let the maids be the proud possessors of
    overflowing chests of hope.

Sandra Harper struggles with disease, art, and life with her daughter in California. She loves life and the world in which she practices the art of living.

DEATH OF A SOLDIER

I don't ask what nationality are you?
What colors are your badges?
Did you die honorably?

I don't ask were the bombs Chinese,
Russian or American, or from what country?
How can I distinguish them,
They destroy all distinctions.

I came in search of you my son.
I have received a few charred ashes
In an urn.
They are ashes . . . .
Are they yours or enemy's I don't ask.
They are ashes.

Prem N. Prasad came from India. She now teaches in a college and pursues her photography hobby.

SOLDIER — — — A PROSE POEM

He approached the dumpster carrying a plastic
Garbage bag filled with the day's refuse.
Overturning the lid, he lifted the load
And hurled it into the bin.

The dumpster was already full,
Being already Friday morning,
So the new load rested atop piles of boxes and
Stuffed garbage bags.

He wiped the grease from the plastic bag
Onto his apron, and he gazed
Into the bin.
He could see dozens of flies crawling and buzzing
Amid the trash, and unconsciously
He asked himself what's the purpose of flies, anyhow?
They're such an annoyance and
Don't really do much!
        They're inhuman, a nuisance;
        A pain.
As he watched two flies copulating on a brown lettuce rib,
He heard a faint, erratic buzz.
Looking to his left, he saw a bluebottle
Trapped in a small area of the plastic bag,
Trying to escape.

It could barely
Move, and buzzed helplessly.
He placed two fingers on the plastic,
Catching the fly
In the grip
Of his thumb
And index finger.
He had never held a fly in his hand before.
Since the little bastards were always so fast,
But for once
He felt the sensation
Of the fly

Buzzing in his grip.
He could feel the fly's fear.
He squeezed gently, and sensed a
Quiet crunch as a curious
White substance oozed
From what looked like the fly's mouth.
He bit his lip
And drew his finger
And thumb
Together,
Forcefully
Grinding the fly's tiny body
Into pulp.

He felt like God.

And he wept.

Timothy P. Strzechowski *teaches composition and research and writes in Chicago.*

COMING HOME

The boys are coming home
from the lands of the world
not knowing what to expect
only hoping for peaceful sleep
and no more pain.
       They return with open hearts
       and open wounds,
       bleeding the red, white and blue
       of a nation
       determined,
       democratic
       and destined to destruct.
       Abused because they killed
       removing the saffron and garnet
       from our Amerikan colour scheme
       and abused if they didn't.
The TV blasts the news
of new conquests
new deaths,
freshly sealed in their
mud baked coffins
but it can only tell us
what it's like
not why.

Patricia Martin Wagstaff is a wife, mother, and bookstore manager. She collects political memorabilia.

THE BATTLE BLOODIES ON

The battle bloodies on while the sun flaps its eyes.
Soldiers spin and stab like mutant
      cancer cells surrounding a solitary nucleus.
The stench increases
           as steam bellows,
released from bloating bellies.

A trumpet sounds.
Time out.

The troops mass 'round,
a football field huddle.
The leader pulls a paper from his bulging black bag.
Pausing, he says with obvious regret,
     It's over.
The Greens are now our allies
           and
it's now the Blues who are the enemy.

A voice echoes throughout the valley of bodies.
But who won . . . won . . . won?

Does it matter . . . matter . . . matter?
the leader retorts, indignant.

It's how you play the game . . . game . . . game.

Sandee Johnson is an artist and photographer who has visited 48 countries.

VALIANT SOLDIERS
(perennials) *

* Please follow planting instructions for your combat zone.

This strain matures at an early 13 years.
Each Valiant Soldier produces guaranteed offshoots
and year after year of hardy kill-resistant stock.

For a good yield work the soil well,
infiltrating it liberally with bone meal and desiccated blood.
Stake supports of barbed wire, digging shallow trenches
along the rows.
Plant the shells at equal intervals with the Soldiers
so they will come up in uniform drills.
Cover the soil and wait for the reign of terror.
Remove and promptly exterminate slugs.
Your crop should advance at the first sign of provocation.

Valiant Soldiers especially thrive on heat,
but will adapt readily to every clime and terrain.
Cut them down to the quick for a continuous supply.

Pests and Diseases:

The bullet fly. The mourning dove. The yellow fungus.
For control of native weed population, spray between drills.
Your grandfather loved Valiant Soldiers so much
he took them Out West! Now, decades later, you
can enjoy the same homegrown riots of khaki.
A continual Presidential choice for monumental
plantings in historic Soldier's Field.
Whether for swamp beds or 6-foot borders
Valiant Soldiers have long been a favorite the world over.

Each shipment government inspected and approved.

Julia Older is a writer who focuses on social and environmental
concerns. She lives in New Hampshire.

VI

War and Children

We Speak for Peace

CHANT FOR OUR CHILDREN

A child can be made
>of words of love
>>of kicks and welts
>for a name
>>for a purpose
>for a web of romantic wishes
>>for the need of muscle and work
>of hot running lust
>>of rape
>to fulfill a dream
>>of trust in a universe
>of a threat
>>to care for a sister or brother
>of a drunken apology
>>to carry a gun
>to finish unfinished work
>>to continue a pattern
>from the dry dust of defeat
>>to consume
>to alter a plan
>>of empty minds
>of intertwined fingers
>>of forest smells
>of rocky cliffs
>>of elegant prams and skyscrapers

A child can be made
and a child can be lost:
body and blood,
sweet sweat and silky hair —

not smoke
not yet, not yet.

*Phyllis Hotch, former teacher of English and Creative Writing,
now tutors GED students in Taos, New Mexico.*

BEYOND VIETNAM

"Is it time for Vietnam?"
I'd ask when I was five.
I thought it was a TV show.

Entranced at twelve by
footage of hippies dancing
long hair flopping
to "Eight Miles High"
painting flowers on their faces in Monterey
Flower power, I told Dad at the dinner table
& he said, Politics
I can live without politics, I said
I hope not, he replied

I tried to piece together
recent history.
Nothing prepared me for this.
Not novels set in the sixties
Dylan or Denise Levertov
Vietnam documentaries
or Hollywood movies
Phil Ochs singing
"I Ain't Marching Anymore"
or Martin Luther King speeches
Granada or Panama

Dad, I am your daughter now
as we chew the war with our dinner
Why didn't you tell me we're
stuck inside history
that politics wouldn't be a choice
but poison in the air
I can't help breathing

Gwynne Garfinkle is a computer clerk, a Jewish feminist, a
poet, and a novelist.

WAR GAME

Pow!
pow! pow! pow!
Pow! pow!"
toy plastic gun
"Pow! pow!" in hand
"Pow!"
smiling
"Pow!"
killing me
"Pow! pow! pow!"

Reeling back
"Pow! pow!"
in pain
"Pow!"
I ask
"Pow!"
Why
"Pow! pow!"
do you want
"Pow! pow!"
to hurt me
"Pow! pow! pow!"
why
"Pow!"
do you want
"Pow!"
to kill
"Pow! pow! pow!"

He answers
"Pow! pow!"
I likta kill people
"Pow! pow! pow!"

James Scrimgeour is *co-founder and co-editor of* Pikestaff
Publications *and teaches at Western Connecticut University.*

YOUNG WAR

the kid has a plastic
tank destroyer
and is pointing it
at the traffic
that rolls endlessly
below his second story window

his mouth makes the
noise of explosions
while his eyes light up
as if each car he aims at
is blown to dust

his mother looks at
him sadly
disgusted at how
big business has put war
in the hands and heads
of children

while his father
remembers wistfully
the times when an open window
a fake weapon
and a slowly moving target
was enough

John Grey: Australian born poet, playwright, short story writer. With his band, "L Shaped Room" performs in various clubs in the Providence area.

TOM MIX AND THE GARDEN OF EDEN

Years ago on Saturday afternoons
I would skip along behind my brother
to the Temple Theater where
we would sit through
action-packed sagas of The Old West.
Tom Mix,
Ken Maynard,
Bill Boyd
were our teachers
of non-attachment to anyone but a horse
and non-allegiance to anything but "what's right."
But the action
would get so fast, so furious and all the fighters
would fight so whole-heartedly
that I would at some point always have to ask my brother,

>"Hey, was that the bad guy?
>*He's* the good guy, isn't he?"

A few years later my brother and I
looked at history books.
World War One was well photographed.
But from the beginning I would get confused.
Searching the faces of Albanians, Hungarians, Serbs
I'd have to ask again,

>"Hey, were these the bad guys?
>Ah, *those* were the bad guys, weren't they
>with the spikes in their helmets!"

My brother didn't answer as quickly
as he did with Ken Maynard and Tom Mix.
One day he got mad at my question
and told me,

"There aren't any all-bad guys
and all-good guys; it's not that simple!"

I didn't ask that question any more.

It wasn't long before World War Two came.
It was action-packed
My brother was one killed in the action
by some guys.

Now everyday encounters
leave me wondering.

Sophie Hughes, *who lost her only brother in World War II,
taught Art at the Lexington School for the Deaf for 25 years.*

We Speak for Peace

AUGUST 1947

Every time the child heard
a plane overhead she ran into
the house, afraid, and afraid
to say she was afraid
because they always said,
calm down,
the war was over two years ago.

But 1947 became '57 and '67—and
when she heard a plane overhead she
imagined rubble where she stood,
and shuddered.

Her father told her nothing of
the war, saying only that
it was too awful to speak of.
Her mother said that when he
first came home her father
dreamed of noise inconceivable,
of British soldiers impaled
on parachute-draped tree limbs,
Germans bloated to bursting,
and Belgian families begging
to peel potatoes for the army.

From 1970 to 1980, deafened by
alcohol, she heard no planes.
When she sobered up her own war
consumed her. All the same, she
stopped and listened when a plane
flew overhead, and shuddered.

That war day in 1991 she heard one
last plane and no longer had to
imagine rubble where she stood.

> **Lee Orcutt Rohwer** is a grandmother, a student in a creative
> writing program, a recovering alcoholic, a recovering perfectionist,
> a political activist, a lovable feminist, and a sort-of vegetarian.

CHILDREN'S STORIES

"Who ordered them to die, who needs it?"
Czeslaw Milosz

At six in the evening
the children spoon their suppers
of stew in the kitchen,
a loud spill of joy above
which you hear
          soldiers—

soldiers, the radio says,
came to a small village of farmers
last night, and attacked a house,
"blew a woman through the floor
of the house, blew a mother-shape hole
in the kitchen floor of the house."
Her four children huddled
by the hole. Their father
lay in the next room, advising
his children how to live
without their mother. All night
his voice
a thread through the thin wall.
All night, the children
listened, huddled,
the four of them, by the hole.
When morning came,
the father was dead.
           the radio
does not tell you

what happens to the children.

At seven in the evening
trees part where the harvest moon
rises, serene mistress of the sun,
and you sit on the couch, a child

close at each side. The story tonight
is *Pinocchio*. The children listen,
knowingly, until it is time
to tuck them in. It is then

you listen

to the wind blowing up from the south,
the wind blowing in from the east, the wind
blowing in from everywhere,
and the wind tells you
stories. Stories of how
hunger pulls the corners of the mouth up
into an uncontrollable smile.
How a rubber bullet in the back
of the head of a five-year-old
produces a blood clot in the brain.
How a land mine gets seven children.
A hand grenade three others.
A booby-trapped toy, another.
Every day. Everywhere
children are dying, or
left orphaned, and homeless, dreaming

of mothers. Fathers. Bread. The story

of life. But, in

this life, this truth
bearer, dark of wing and long of tooth,
tells you—unlike Pinocchio, unlike
children,
soldiers have forgotten how to dream
of redemption. In this life
soldiers are taught
it is not the business of soldiers
to dream,
it is the business of soldiers to write

the stories of children,

and
there is no rescue—
no rescue from these stories,
until you learn

the names of your children. Until

you learn the names of your children.

Regina deCormiero-Skekerjian is a writer whose abiding
concerns are peace and human rights.

"the wicked are trapped by the works of their own hands,"
Ps. 9:16

pediatric emergency

for maura, ita, jean, dorothy,
chalatenango, el salvador
2 December 1980

victims of war
occupy these beds
a city's children wounded from birth
fix vigilant gaze at shadows
that pass that do not stop

a young veteran
threads a white sheet through the bars
of his crib. practices taking hostages
practices feeling safe. feeling brave
he repeats his name **chichiri y tengo tres anitos.**
like a song, **chi-chir-ri,** a solitary song bird
chichiri-isaiah alone in a cage

in a darkened room

at home three generations live cramped in two
barely furnished rooms; meals are taken
at the window sill, watching the soaps, watching
the street occupied and ready for action

children play. adults
are outnumbered. **tukuru, sapito, chati, bimbi**
awilda-flor. abuela knows this
is the inheritance she may outlive

daughters, nieces, *prima*
hasta las nietas lost

to the street. fathers of their children
assumed dead. cheap chemical explosives

bazooka, uzis, crack, *sida,* bad deals
bad blood

families with casualties on both sides
cypress and 141st. third world. our border

babies wake, craving
the familiar breast, the soothing voice
of one whose hands are trained
to resist the battle, to end this war

south bronx/1989

Deborah L. Humphreys is a Sister of Charity who is the Director
of a Family Resource Center in Newark, New Jersey. She has
worked for 20 years in New York's South Bronx and the Lower
East Side.

SAVE THE CHILDREN

I am a child of the
      Sandanista in Nicaragua
A young guerrilla in the
      cloud forests of Africa
A student insurgent in the
      halls of Granada
Rebellious children among
      the starving of Ethiopia
A Kurdish child sleeping
      forever in the arms of
      my father in Halabja
A rock throwing teenager
      in Palestine
A child of the IRA growing
      up on the streets of
      Belfast
Children of diamond miners
      in South Africa
Winter's child of the
      homeless in America
My greatest wish is that my
      generation will grow up
      strong and free from the
      yoke of oppression
And that we will not follow
      the teachings of war
      of our parents . . .

John B. Passerello works for the California Office of Emergency Services involving earthquakes, fires, floods and other major disasters. He is also a volunteer with the Salvation Army.

HANA'S PANTOUM

I am fifteen months old
I know nothing of war or bombs
My name is Hana, daughter of Khadafy
though I do not know these words

I know nothing of war or bombs
I know warm milk, pink dresses, Mama's soft cheek
though I do not know these words
I am just learning how to walk

I know warm milk, pink dresses, Mama's soft cheek
the safety of darkness pinpointed with stars
I am just learning how to walk
on my chubby legs, my feet in little white shoes

The safety of darkness pinpointed with stars
One night the whole world exploded. There was red water
on my chubby legs, my feet in little white shoes
I never learned the word for blood

One night the whole world exploded. There was red water
I wanted to make a picture with the pretty color
I never learned the word for blood
But my fingers were gone and so was my hand

I wanted to make a picture with the pretty color
Big splotches all over my dress
But my fingers were gone and so was my hand
I didn't even have time to cry

Big splotches all over my dress
I could have been a famous painter or a movie star
I didn't even have time to cry
My Mama cries all the time now, I can hear her

I could have been a famous painter or a movie star
Maybe I would have looked just like my Mama

My Mama cries all the time now, I can hear her
calling my name, remembering my dark eyes

Maybe I would have looked just like my Mama
I wish my Mama was here now
calling my name, remembering my dark eyes
that no longer see and no longer cry

I wish my Mama was here now
There's lots of little children here
that no longer see and no longer cry
Most of them aren't famous like me

There's lots of little children here
They all want someone to write a poem about them
Most of them aren't famous like me
Children from South Africa, children from Nicaragua

They all want someone to write a poem about them
Weave their names into a chain to wrap around the earth
Children from South Africa, children from Nicaragua
shattered into a million pieces like stars

Weave their names into a chain to wrap around the earth
I am fifteen months old
shattered into a million pieces like stars
My name is Hana, daughter of Khadafy

Lesléa Newman *writes and lives in Northampton,
Massachusetts.*

THE ROOTS OF PACIFISM

When I was nine, I was in the fourth grade, along with Selene Castellacci, who was new, and Anne Carson, whom I had hated since second grade with a soul-destroying passion because she was prettier than I was, and before she came I had been the prettiest. We three were the entire fourth grade at Deepriver Elementary School, where we shared a room and a teacher with the first, second, and third grades. The other four grades inhabited the room across the hall, and were taught by our teacher's husband.

We studied World History, which consisted of Greek myths and Christian-devouring lions, mostly, and Geography, in which we were taught that Africa and South America had certainly never been near each other, even though it looked as if they had if one were a foolish child. I had a lot of trouble with short division and with multiplying by ten or one hundred, but I enjoyed Art. Mr. Webster would draw a picture and show us all how to copy it exactly. We studied Music. The rest of the fourth grade got to go to the other room of the school and learn how to play Tonettes, but I had proven quite hopeless in Band, and was relegated to playing the piano for the primary grades. I was not sure if this were a disgrace or an honor.

At lunch time we would all go into the playground and segregate ourselves more or less by age, starting with the first-graders beside the front steps, into a string of ever-taller children leading all the way around the school to the eighth grade's playground beside the driveway. The fourth grade's territory extended from the merry-go-round to the row of cottonwoods in the southwest corner of the school yard. We played with the fifth grade in the south and the younger kids in the north.

In the winter of that year I formed a club which consisted of me, and Selene, and most of the third grade, and Billy Gahr, who was older by two or three years and had flunked once, or had some similar vague disgrace attached to him. My club had no particular purpose except possibly to exclude Anne Carson.

But Anne formed her own club, and the entire rest of the school joined it, and most of the third grade deserted, except my sister, and Billy Gahr admitted that he was in my club just so he could be a spy for her club. So we had a war, and for about a month we sat in our separate camps just out of earshot and glared and plotted.

My club dug a foxhole big enough to hold all of us, about two feet deep. The other group had too many people to fit in our foxhole, but Billy Gahr, who had agreed to be a double agent, reported plans to attack it, anyway. Every once in a while we would chase away a scout they had sent sneaking through the cottonwoods.

The war was more important to many people than anything else, and no one who was in one club spoke to anyone who was in the other. Except Billy Gahr. This disrupted the classroom and so the war became important to Mrs. Webster, who made Anne and I shake hands and break up our clubs and agree to peace, and made all of us stop the war.

Nothing could make me stop hating Anne Carson.

| **Ruby R. Muran de Asserito** *lives and writes in San Francisco.*

NEWS REPORT

Did you see the children
with sparkling dark eyes
and smiling round faces
staring at the camera
while around them lays
the rubble
that once was their home.

*Jean Kemper is an environmentalist, a recent widow, a
grandmother, a traveler, a gourmet cook, and an activist.*

ENGLISH AS A FOREIGN LANGUAGE

The teacher writes *war.*
One pupil, finding it hard
to say the letter "r,"
accidentally asks, *why?*
One of the orphans starts to cry.
This, the teacher thinks, is more
than I bargained for.

Forging a new language
is the first campaign.
Those who have learned
catch as catch can,
caught at a disadvantage,
need to have
the simplest things explained.

Men are no longer men,
women no longer women.
Children over *here* remain
children, while others, made
into collateral damage,
grub through rubble
or shiver in the dark, afraid.

The teacher writes, *war.*
A pupil well on her way
(but not yet *there)*
accidentally asks, *where?*
The orphans all keep quiet.
This, the teacher thinks,
is more like it.

I *J. Kates is a translator and a poet.*

VALENTINES FOR SOLDIERS

At the mission school in Española
the children cut out hearts
and write their messages of love.
My daughter, Hope, among them
learning to cut and paste with urgency.

These days, she cries more.
Follows me around after dark.
She goes back in time, fights more
with her brother, clings.
I think it's the war.

My older friend agrees.
Her children's children are the same,
and so is she, grandmotherly,
yet, uncertain how to grow
in this blitzed face of peace.

Their letters to the president didn't work.
No one listened to Hope's voice.
She sends valentines to soldiers,
concentrates, pastes paper lace
onto a red heart.

Joan Logghe, Poetry Editor for Mothering Magazine, *lives with her husband in a solar home they built themselves in Española, New Mexico.*

FOR ALL THE CHILDREN

Magnets hold the Weekly Reader
map of the Middle East
on one side
of a metal cabinet.
The concept of continents—
an essential element
in our curriculum—hard, though
for second graders.
I say name your country,
they say Texas. But they begin
to understand a little
now that Senisa's father
has gone to war.
He sends coins with Arabic
writing and the face of an emir.
He speaks of oil slicks, never
scuds. Doesn't like
the heat, says the desert
is unpleasant. The children
tell him what they are learning:
how to count money,
how to read maps,
how to decode—
deal with diphthongs and digraphs,
how to make present tense
past. One child writes
about a lesson on words
with multiple meanings—*note*,
trip, frame, point, light, soil,
right.

Vera Banner *has lived in Nigeria (during the Biafran War),
Kuwait, and Indonesia.*

BODY BAG

Mom, what does a body bag
look like?

Where did she hear that word?
Body bag.

She's been drawing pictures
peace signs in each

corner. One large peace sign
fills the center of the page.

No to War
Yes to Peace

Now she wants to add

something new. It's green,
I say, not forest green,

more yellowish-brown
Kind of dull. It's

rectangular and has a zipper
up the middle. Yes, like

a sleeping bag, but
not so tapered.

It's made of heavy slick
— my skin shrinks at the remembered
feel of the cold slickness —
plastic and has

two handles on each side
so they can pick it up.

She draws
a body bag in red

ink. No, green I say.
This one,

she replies, has
a body in it.

Carolyn S. Scarr has been a peace and justice activist for many years, basing her life and her activities in Berkeley, California.

WAR-GONE

I was not seasoned by my father,
who went to war unbidden,
and reckless, flowed a blood river.
I wanted to tear his star-eyes,
rip him from my mother's tears,
shake him off over the compost heap,
and bid the worms consume
his betrayal of me.

C.B. Follett *lives in Sausalito, California, where she owns and operates a ceramics company.*

WAR

I have young-men sons, and you are talking war.
I have sons sweeping their paths, licking at life,
and you are war whooping through the halls of power.
My sons newly free, are making plans,
and you are out-flanking them with sand and drums.

I raised my sons to care, and you want them to kill.
I urged them towards compassion, tolerance.
You would dehumanize them into engines of death.

You face a monster in the sands; he sees the same.
You say he will not budge; he says it of you,
and there, he's just as right. Turn your face
from these young men, and look within.
Despite your need to flex, to snarl, to save face,
pick one of the other solutions.

TROOP LIFTS SHATTER AUGUST SKIES
Bush Comments from Golf Cart in Kennebunkport

8/90: Okay. You look at it your way
I'll look at it mine: If you ask me it's damn scary
how much we seem to want war. As if peace
isn't purpose enough. Don't talk to me about patriotism
I'm a child of Two: veteran of 365 x 3 and $^1/2$ years
of *Now I lay me . . . please bring daddy home safe*
from the wars. Ask me about anger about fear
how it was when he came back. Ask me about parades
in our town the peeling red white and blue sign
in the yard of the Enfield church that says he was a son
who fought for them. Ask me about the wine
the horrors he couldn't talk about but punished
us with. Ask how the Star Spangled Banner chokes me
ours folded tri-like in her china closet just like
that war centered our lives. Just like she fought too.
Ask me about the measure of a man's life: medals divided
five ways. Ask me about military funerals
standard issue markers set flat for easy mowing
stonecutters working 'round the clock hundreds
from that war dying every day. *Welcome sons and daugh-*
ters the Legionnaires say when we come. They know. Ask
my kids what I've said their grandfather fought for what it
meant. Then we'll talk patriotism nothing to do with oil.

Patricia Ranzoni, *education consultant and mental health counselor, lives with her husband and their woodland friends on a homestead in Maine.*

LOSING

I was in the bathroom, probably fixing my make-up like teenagers do when my father walked toward that prop jet to Saigon. Maybe he turned around and looked for me; I don't know. I stood at the gate and watched, but the passengers and crew had finished boarding. The plane seemed so huge that a crew would need a lift just to shut the baggage compartment door. Then a man walked over and reached up to close the hatch. The plane was small, too small to carry my father. The man rolled away the steps. A propeller started spinning. My father was going. A baggage cart snaked by. The other propeller started. A man with headsets waved neon flashlights. The plane started to move. My father was really going. It trundled across the pavement to the runway. The plane disappeared behind a pole. My father was almost gone. Larger planes took off. My father's plane whirred down the runway and hung in the air, suspended. It grew smaller and took on the gray of the sky. Once it caught the sun's glint, a sequin. I blinked; the sky stretched on alone. My father was gone.

For years after we buried the Army-issue coffin that they said held his body, I searched faces of returning POW's on the news. Once an MIA reported dead came home. I watched this pale soldier descend from a plane onto American dirt. You see, I never saw my father dead. I asked the funeral director to open the lid of that gray casket, but he said no. My father's body was in pieces. This is what Vietnam made of him, made of us.

Lynne Conroy, a graduate student at Harvard, lost her father in the Vietnam war.

KAMAKURA

I don't recall when I first understood
why you stiffen at the roar of low flying jets—

Did you tell me, mother, or did I just know somehow?
When you refused to show me the caves like
eyes in the hills behind Bah-chan's house—

Did I only dream it, how when the sirens began the trains
stopped
dead in their tracks, unleashing a stream of thousands to
rush
blind and headlong toward those sheltering hills—

the damp press of strange bodies in darkness
rank with the stench of war's leavings?
Only imagine a young girl's cries drowned in the tumult,
the urgent gropings of unseen hands—

the bombs raining on Yokohama Harbor all through
the night, hothouse blooms crackling in a seething sky,
then hissing into a boiling sea—

Was it a millennium that passed before the sirens ceased
their wailings,
only to be taken up again by the dogs and the dying

But you talk of none of this today. We walk slowly,
saying little, as if less said will keep the heat at bay—
The air is wet, heavy with summer smells
carried aloft on the hypnotic drone of cicadas

You show me where as a girl you played in other summers,
catching *kabuto* beetles and dragonflies in bamboo cages

What must go through you when we pass them
at a distance, those black maws yawning out of the hillside,
exhaling the unspeakable.

Mari L'Esperance *is the daughter of a Japanese mother and a French-Canadian American father. This poem is about her mother's experience during World War II in Japan.*

F TRAIN

A pig-tailed girl carefully irons out
a Ring-Ding wrapper with a penny
and proudly displays a flawless
piece of aluminum foil to her mother.
A New York Post headline barks out
across the aisle of war and Scuds
and oil-slick ducks,
I envision slow-moving camels
filled with disgust.

And babies in gas mask
building Tinker-Toy towns
and on target high-fives
against holy wars
and where's Bob Hope
when you need a good laugh?

Outside the subway window,
glue factories and smokestacks
dawdle by and how thankful I am
for the pink neon Kentile sign
still flickering away over Brooklyn.

I *Lori Horvitz works in the graphic-arts field in New York City.*

THE NEWS AS HEARD BY A CHILD

The News is on the TV
    My forehead forms a frown.
I sit smaller, tighter, more tense
    A pleasant face says, "Child, two, drowns."

Shootings, crashes, floods of lava
    Poison pills, a huge earthquake;
As the list of terrors lengthens
    I can feel my insides shake.

Will the killer find my window?
    Bombs fall on me from the sky?
Cars crash into my own school yard?
    Or a baseball smash my eye?

I see photographs of soldiers
    And I wonder where they'll fight;
I see wounded children, crumpled homes
    And noon times turned to night.

The world out there attacks me
    The News stings my ears and eyes.
I want a world that's safer,
    People kinder, no kids die.

Marilyn Radinsky Deak has worked as a clinical child psychologist for 25 years. She lives with her own three children in Wilmington, Delaware.

SCHOOL PARENT COUNCIL MEETING
UNDER THE GEORGE BUSH CONTROLLED CHOICE PLAN

The first half-hour we sit mute, until
someone reads an agenda.
Slow-motion robots, words
shuffle from our mouths. *Item:*
given textbook funds insufficient for students in
all grades, for which grades must funds
definitely be set aside? Numbed we listen, argue
scrambling to control a pencil mark on a
line item. *Decision: grades 3 through 5*
definitely need one textbook per child. Tonight we
gag over this task, war blitzkrieging
across television screens as we left our homes.
a billion dollars a day to carpet bomb Iraq
a billion dollars a day to uphold monarchy
Our children: beggars for books and
don't ask for art supplies next year.
How many candy bars how many 5 cent deposit on bottles
how many grocery stubs to collect cookies to sell
pizza slices: cut them in half to make extra!
A billion dollars a day to carpet bomb Iraq?
A billion dollars a day to uphold monarchy?
A mother's curse on you George Bush!
We spit on your choices, your mocking of us.
Yellow ribbon down your throat!

Susan Eisenberg is a Boston-based union electrician, performer,
teacher, and tradeswoman activist.

FANTASIA

I dream
of
giving birth
to
a child
who will ask,
"Mother,
what
was
war?"

Eve Merriam supported herself and her children by writing poems and plays in New York City. We mourn her death in 1992.

VII

War and Women

WOMAN'S WAR POEM 1991

From ten thousand miles away
we could feel the heat rising,
the rocketing levels of testosterone
as more than one million men
squared off in the sand.
O God, couldn't they all,
generals, politicians,
grunts and all,
just brandish their dicks
and jack off all at once,
dick to dick,
eyeball to eyeball,
spilling their killing seed
on the ground instead
of each other's blood.

Katherine Wells *is a mixed media sculptor who also does performance and installation art. She is involved in Green Politics.*

WARRIORS

We are the dispossessed of war, nameless victims,
　　　forgotten casualties.
We are the dispossessed, the waiters, the mourners,
　　　the ones who clean the bodies, wash away the signs
of dying,
　　　sanitize the traces of death.
We who hold the body close to us in the dying,
　　　as we held the body close in life,
　　　smelled the baby sweetness,
　　　the young boy sweatyness,
　　　the young man perfumed and flowered gone in
search of love.
We who are women:
　　　mother, daughter, sister, cousin, friend, wife and
lover
　　　who are left behind, who wait behind,
　　　　　clinging to a last memory, a picture in the
mind,
　　　　　a photo of a body upright,
　　　　　tall and strong, smiling, frowning, scowling,
handsome, cute,
　　　　　flirtatious, devil, shy, imp,
　　　　　the photo etched in the metal of our mind,
　　　　　a plate left to capture and to hold,
　　　　　an image gone, clung to, held close, held dear.

The women throw themselves across the coffin,
　　　weeping, across the coffin,
　　　throw themselves across metal or wood, stone or
straw.
　　　The coffin comes in many forms, in any form,
　　　what is available, what is:
　　　Poncho liner, body bag, burlap, piece of rag,
　　　whatever is, is handy, is available, is used,
　　　wrapped around, wrapped over, lift and carry.
　　　The body does not care; dead is dead.
The women throw themselves across the coffin,
　　　across the grave, across the stone,

We Speak for Peace

throw themselves,
reaching out for contact, reaching out for flesh,
warm flesh, flesh and pulsing, moving, flowing blood.
The women reach for one last touch,
one last warm, human touch,
and find the cold hardness of the coffin wall,
the graveside wall, the granite Wall.
The women cry,
their tears flowing down cheeks drawn and dry with
age and waiting,
cheeks hot and burning with emotions,
with grief and pain and sorrow and rage.

We are the dispossessed of war.
We, the women: the mothers, daughters, sisters, cousins,
friends,
lovers and wives.
We, who wait and learn our fate only when it is too late to
change it,
who wait and learn only when it is time to wail and
mourn
and send our sons, fathers, brothers, cousins,
friends, lovers
and husbands
beyond their end of war.

We are the silent casualties of war.
We who are left behind, protected,
left to be protected, to be left protected,
to be kept back, safe and protected,
whether we want to or not;
we who do not choose protection
but have protection thrust upon us,
we who will be kept safe, at sanctuary,
who will be kept behind,
whether we want to or not.

We are not safe. We are not protected. We are not
sanctuary.
Our bodies become the battleground when our side has
fallen.

We become the new territory to conquer, to use,
        to rape and plunder, to tear apart,
        to bomb, burn, riddle with bullet holes and destroy.
We who are protected become the battleground of war.

We are not safe. We are not protected. We are not sanctuary.
Our bodies become the battleground even when our side
has won.
We become the delivered territory to welcome home the
heroes,
        hot and sweaty and eager, energy high and flowing,
ready,
        needing release, a place to flow, a place for letting go.
        In us.
        Liberated territory.
        Live heroes.
And when we are not the earth in which the warriors bury
their
                energy from war,
Then we are left at last and alone
        to bury the warriors
        in an earth of soil and grass.
We are the earth and hole in which the warrior buries
himself,
Or we will dig the hole in earth in which to bury the warrior
                ourselves.

We are the dispossessed of war,
        the silent causalties of war,
        the nameless victims burying dearly named, closely
held warriors
        over and over and over again.
We are the ghosts that move up after the rage has passed.
We are the waters filling in the spaces,
        closing the hallow gaps,
        seeping into pockets,
        and washing away, washing clean.
We are the grass, growing up and over,

hiding the scars,
disguising the signs,
blurring the lines,
easing the pain,
smudging the boundaries,
and cleaning away the traces of death and dying and
the destruction of war.

We are the dispossessed, the victims, the casualties.
We are the unnamed, the unaccounted for, the unnoticed,
unwanted, unsung.
We are the women.
We are the Warriors.
We are the water, the grass, the ghosts.
We are the ones left behind.
We are the ones who weep and clean and bury and
      in little pieces
      without glory
      finally
      die.

Julia Starzky works for the Massachusetts Department of Mental Retardation. She believes that "the art of creating peace must be reflected in the way we live our lives . . . every day."

NIKITA

Under a heavy wire milk case,
A piece of concrete foundation
On top, in summer, in her backyard,
Mrs. Russo keeps the cat Nikita safe
From birds, from dogs, from eating
Johnson grass, which he throws up.
Nikita waits for ants to wander in
And for the sun to leave.
Instead, she comes to keep him
Company, saying you look fat
And that her son died,
Remember I told you?
Walking thin in his uniform
On a road.

*Alberto Alvaro Rios is a Professor of English at Arizona State
University.*

WAR WIDOW

Every winter she waits behind the reception desk,
typing away white paper,
letter by letter;
waiting out the snow.

She spends her summers collecting sea shells:
blue, white, red;
on any suntanned beach held by the sea
that also holds her lover.

H. Edgar Hix is a legal secretary with the Stillwater, Oklahoma Legal Aid Office. He lives in a mobile home with his wife and three cats.

DOVETAIL

Odd to have a student in a war.
Not brother or son, no
blood
ties, but nonetheless
a bond.

The mother speaks to her son
one last time
whispers warm words
that tickle his ear
on explosive nights.

The teacher, an outsider,
intimate by chance and by choice,
faces the thought of his
death
alone
restrained from status
from wording her own good-bye.

On occasion, the mother and teacher
meet and speak with
conscious control born of
terror.
The mother battles
planning for hope
planning for grief
absorbed by the conflict.

The teacher watches, listens, nods,
knows she has no rights
to a child
of her mind.

The student's letters recommence,
youthful tales of distant missiles
and flagrant games

played in the sand.
He contemplates his future
which is
as it should be.

The mother gives thanks
with relieved assurance.
The teacher remembers
the mother's fear
her own
the student's face
and feels used.

I *Anne Giles Rimbey* is a teacher and writer in Tampa, Florida.

FOR A SON ON THE PERSIAN GULF

In the Sixties a huge glass peace sign
hung on the beam in our living room.
We didn't allow you to have toy guns or G.I. Joes.
Your best friend was a girl. You went fishing together,
sold lemonade on hot afternoons.
I showed you how to make origami cranes,
sent you to your room if you hit your brother.
Once, when I found you in the back yard,
staring down at a frog you'd killed,
I made you bury it and say a prayer.

Now I worry that you don't have the killer instinct,
that you'll be standing in the desert somewhere,
and there will be that second
when you look away from the enemy line
and up at the sky, at the clouds I taught you to name.

Forgive me. I raised you for peace.

*Sondra Upham, retired, is the volunteer poet-in-residence at
Duxbury High School. She also runs a poetry workshop at the
retirement community in Duxbury, Massachusetts.*

SYMBOLS AND SALUTES

Her youngest travelled
                from her body
and is gone before her going.
        Her mind is occupied with loss.
                How comprehend a jungle
and a shore so different.

        A gold star
                a triangled flag
                        held against
her breast is no exchange for his small warm wriggle.

        These symbols
                and salutes
                        and bugle calls
                and crisp commands register
in morning's slanted light
        where they lie all of them
                sons of mothers, husbands of wives.

        Her grief harbors young men
                harvested on strange soil
cut never to rise nor wake
        soft and smelling of sleep.
                Her memory
                        cradles him
as the bugle sounds.

Emma Landau spends her life in the world of art and poetry in New York City.

20,000 YEARS OF MOTHERS

I am a woman, weary of birthing death.
Weary of weaning life from my womb,
beautiful, pulsing, laughing life,
that too soon lies limp, riddled with war.

Son of my son,
daughter of my grand daughter,
soul of my soul, flesh of my bone,
earth of my birth,
all despoiled, dead.
How I long to cradle your soft,
fleshy bodies in my arms.

Oh, arms of war,
listen to the mothers who sob alone at night,
hoping for an ear to hear,
a heart to listen.
"We would not have you kill for oil or soil or power or . . ."

Even tears cannot refresh wasted, weary, wombs
shrunken by so much grief.
Earth is furrowed by gullies of salt and blood,
worn barren to 20,000 years,
and still.

Joan Brown (Order of St. Francis) lives in a home that offers shelter to women in need, works at a local soup kitchen, and takes part in a local political theatre troupe in Colorado Springs.

BEIRUT: FIRE-FREE ZONE

War is the greatest plague that can afflict humanity. It
destroys . . . . states, it destroys families. Any scourge is
preferable to it.

                                    Martin Luther

Black flags of mourning
cling like cobwebs in attics,
hindering movement; the wails
of grieving women
pierce the air.

Five small
stone abodes
lay flattened
by explosives
as human forms jut
in obscene fragments
amidst fiery debris.

A single woman,
frightened and alone,
stares disbelieving
at the upturned faces
of three mute sons
lying heaped as rubble
between her feet,
shock frozen firmly
behind their eyes . . .

I *Pearl Bloch Segall lives and writes in Warren, Ohio.*

BATTLEGROUND

Stop
praising pinpoint accuracy,
tracing the war on impromptu bedsheet maps,
dropping bombs in our conversation,
conjuring fighter planes into my dreams.

"Who could argue
with such a beautiful war?"
you say half-joking,
half-serious,
and I remember
spilled tea spreading
a dark stain across our quilt,
purple-streaked funeral flowers,
tattooed numbers
on your cleaning lady's arm.

You have called my body,
these rounded breasts,
strong thighs, softly curving stomach,
        —beautiful—
has my flesh,
this sweet and solid shell,
become a battleground,
soft desert terrain giving way under pressure?

We used to touch in daylight,
fill Sunday afternoons
with our bodies.

Now, as you grope towards me in the dark,
how can I explain
the clutch in the stomach,
the rippling shiver,
the instinctive rush of fear?

How can I tell you?

(my whole body vibrates
                no
pulsates
                wrong wrong wrong)

You wonder why I push you away—

Bridget Meeds raises funds for a senior citizens' home, grows vegetables and listens to opera in Ithaca, New York.

WOMEN IN THE SERVICE

"Top sent me," the girl said.
"Top told me to be here."

Under the sheet, her knees made circles,
thighs pressed flat, breasts tipped
to the sides.

You took off your pants,
arranged her for entry.
When you came, she called you Sir.

Sallie Bingham of Kentucky is a writer and the founder of The
American Voice Journal *and of the Wolf Pen Artists' Colony.*

MOBILIZATION

I

A month before mobilization
my daughter lies beside me and talks
the way she did at naptime
when she was three.

When I groan I need to sleep
she pats my stomach
and sings the tuneless lullaby
my mother sang to me:

Like blinds my eyes flash open: How
does she know it? She laughs, chattering
in that tongue she never learned.

II

The night before her mobilization
friends came to say goodbye
as if she were embarking on a long journey.

But there is only a kitbag, 3 pairs
of socks, long underwear
and a funny doll
God knows
where she will hide.

III

"Women belong
in the same jobs as men,"
she retorts when the Rabbi on TV
calls for a demobilization of all women
from the army. Then "Men belong
in the same jobs as women,
in their homes, in the kitchen,
in safe places
away from the borders."

Karen Alkalay-Gut teaches poetry at Tel Aviv University. Her two daughters have completed their service in the Israeli Army; her son will begin his next year.

NAVAL RESERVE NURSE

My little girl Sally   always plays nurse
To her Barbie and Ken dolls
Not pretty clothes but Band-Aids and iodine
Cover her dolls' bodies

She's just a little brown-eyed   dark-haired girl
Who wears her toy stethoscope around her neck
Like a fine piece of jewelry

From her childhood days on
Marilyn knows what her career will be
She becomes a Registered Nurse at age 21
She works in Pediatrics   her arms are filled with
Babies and young children that
She loves and cares for

She has more talent and time
Than her work calls for
So with stethoscope in hand
She enlists as a Naval Reserve Nurse

Three months later Sally   is called up
For duty in Saudi Arabia
I cried   no   no   darling   don't go

I must go, Mother, Sally   said
I must help care for the wounded
The war will be over fast
I'll be home for Christmas
All the wise men say so
You just wait and see

I write many letters to my little girl
I receive one from her
She says she is fine
That she will be home for Christmas

Then nothing

Yesterday, an official wire arrives
It says   We are sorry to inform you
That your daughter was killed
By a Scudd missile last night

Now I dust her room
I see her stethoscope on the dresser
I pick it up   I cradle it in my arms
And rock it back and forth

Dorothy L. Rose lives, paints and writes in Westlake Village, California.

VIII

Nuclear Weapons

We Speak for Peace

THE FIRST TEST

I saw the first flash of the secret test
from Bald Mountain on a midsummer night,
when the deep black sky around me was shattered
by splinters of light that zigzagged in all directions,
as if the dome of heaven had cracked and a hand
scribbles mad letters of fire across the sky.
I could not understand the strange display;
three weeks later the world heard from Hiroshima.*

"Lo, I have become Death, the destroyer of worlds,"
the chief tester at Yucca Flat quoted the Vedas . . .
How will man use his new promethean prize?
Too much has he learned, yet too little for wisdom;
too steep the step before him, by a thousand years;
too early, too soon, our lad's not yet ripe for it.

I did not know what I was witnessing,
alone on a midsummer night in the wilderness:
Whom could I warn in a tardy lookout's report?
Now everyone knows yet few seem to understand.
Now men are chained to the new idols they built
and forge the future by old altars of fear,
transmuting the strange power in the elements
but never transmuting the stranger heart of man.

They learned to steal the fire that burns in the sun;
they can teach a lump of clay to bury a city.
But which of them can build a blade of grass,
invent a bird, or teach the unraveling atoms
to clothe a valley of radiant bones in flesh
and raise dead children to walk a green earth again?

Nuclear Weapons

* The first atom bomb was detonated at Yucca Flat, Nevada, on July 16, 1945, and its refractions reached across the Sierra Nevadas as far as Bald Mountain and beyond; on August 6, an atom bomb was dropped on Hiroshima, killing 100,000 men, women and children.

Cornel Adam Lengyel, *born in 1915, famed poet and writer, saw the flash from the first A-bomb test while employed as a fire lookout on Bald Mountain in northern California by the U.S. Forest Service in 1945.*

THE POST-TRINITY PARTY UP ON MAGIC MOUNTAIN
LOS ALAMOS, N.M. JULY 16, 1945

Rumors were that the atmosphere
itself would be set on fire
Fermi thought that all life
might be destroyed, possibly
just New Mexico, but
the test was a 20,000 TNT
equivalent success

Oppenheimer in his scientific,
mystical fashion
quoted the Bhagavad Gita
"I am become Death," he said
"the Shatterer Of Worlds"
Major Groves just joked, it was
"brighter than two stars,"
pointing at his insignia of rank
exploding for promotion
While gooseflesh stood on some
thinking of God's creation,
"Let there be light!" was His command

Plutonium laden clouds
began to drift towards Vaughn,
112 miles to the north of the site,
they arrived just as the night
was falling

Back at home base
celebration had already begun
Banging garbage lids together,
playing Taos Pueblo drums
Drinking, back-slapping
congratulations including
a Snake Dance that wound
coiling and uncoiling
through the streets
till dawn

Kitty* sat and drank,
refilling her glass
Tossing it back,
swallowing hard
it went down,
and down
and down

*Kitty Oppenheimer, wife of Julius, U.S. physicist who
headed the Manhattan Project

A.K. Baumgard, a housewife in Taos, New Mexico, has been
worried about nuclear holocaust since 1950. A peace activist,
she has one husband, three children and two dogs.

ENOLA GAY

Cobblestones threaten underfoot
as I jog past the red brick house
where we lived when the Enola Gay
released the A-Bomb. We celebrated peace
never a thought to those
yellow bodies, poisoned and burned
by the fire-ball.

I cut through the cemetery
crew-cut grass, cypress trees at attention.
Shouts from a protesters' march on Main Street
and police sirens fill the air. I halt,
Asian faces scramble before me. I remember,
it was a Monday, before laundry whitened clotheslines,
that the bomb fell, August 6, 1945,

its belly full of radiating fire
to crack open the earth, disintegrate
like shooting stars
these small formal people at tea ceremonies
and return their bowing ashes
to a pathless earth
in pitchy darkness.

I hear protesters screaming,
see them running. I run too, stumble on a dark blind world
where people consume people,
their bones threatening underfoot
their ashes falling everywhere.

Savina Roxas was born and bred in New York City. A former
librarian, she now lives, writes and studies in Pittsburgh,
Pennsylvania.

VISITING HIROSHIMA

Hundreds of huge, full-ripened roses,
Tomato red and blush pink, surround
The perpetual flame that flits
With the shifting wind in Peace Park.
Inside the museum, photos
Show the black-charred half-bodies
Of children, the rubble-strewn moonscape
Of a town flattened by 5400 degrees,
The remains of the vaporized—shadowy
Tattoos, grilled to the street.
A flash and the flesh melts, sloughs
Off the bones in clumps, while the trace
That escapes burns a swath across the horizon,
Shrieks. The President, obsolete
As his vaunted missile "Peacekeeper,"
Urges a shield in space—to resist,
He insists, not inflict, penetration.
A popular line. It fails.
Ask a sixteen-year-old.
Penetration is too appealing.
A single exchange could establish
A grand museum, a showcase for human
Extinction, with skeletons well preserved,
As regal as bones left extant
By that early invasion, when a white-hot
Fireball shrouded the earth in flames
And sunlight-choking soot,
Felling the despot Tyrannosaurus
And his foes, the end of an empire.

*Michele Wolf, award winning poet, now writes for magazines.
Her work appears in* When I Am an Old Woman I Shall Wear
Purple, *Papier Maché Press.*

NUCLEAR PREPAREDNESS

Shall I compare us to a summer's day
poised frail, improbable, between two winters,
chronicled—for the final, sputtering aeons
of this spinning rock—
only in the memory of crickets?

Mother of God, who ever knew such regret
as ours for our lemmings' pell-mell rush,
for the eclipse of life, the ravaging of God
that we can barely still reverse?
We here in the dappling sun, the morning breeze,
in the shade of all our treasured monuments
to this exquisite garden—
we, so ingeniously prepared,
are paralyzed by our own brainchild.

Were there primordial blueprints
for blasting it all away
at the slip of a hair trigger?

Yes, we have them. And plan to use them.
We, the summer's day.

The rocks show this:
Early comets pulverized Earth's crust
and brought unending winter
to no creature that remembered summer.

Cloud-dust belts ringed the earth, miles-thick,
guaranteed temperatures too low for life,
trapped the water in ice,
shielded the ceremony of total night
with its procession of extinctions.

This is the Nuclear Winter.

It will cancel
three-and-a-half billion years
(There is a prospect of fossils.)

Nuclear Weapons

But we are not listening to our own voices.

Trading is brisk today in extinctions.
Fossils in business suits
sell tin guided futures in MAD.*
The upscale young go into designing Trident,
their fringe benefits yet to come:
spacious lawns of radioactive ash.
My Johnny, who knows, says hell-no to college.
He won't be here that long.
Johnny—
     Sarah—
          Absalom, my small son!
If I were king, the robot men would still cut you down.

What can I do?

What *can* I do?

I can:

(1)	Organize.	What? A world-scale summit for parents with horrible dreams.
(2)	Publicize:	That all the dreams come to the same. That our greed is after all less than our terrified love.
(3)	Vandalize:	Hack up the missiles, with on-site inspection, picnics, and prison; new waves of parents; new waves of jailings; new parents.

Inconvenient? Nuclear war
is convenient?

One of my dreams:

We Speak for Peace

An explosion deafens the landscape.
The huge cloud looms, leering with poison.
My city gashes open
to scenes from Hieronymus Bosch.
Terra firma boils.
Sheets of fire twist around
what I hope are corpses.
In my belly and brain, cancers race
to a gamma counter gone berserk.
There is no balm
for anything.

I've wrapped my child
in a water-soaked bedsheet.
He used to be heavy; I run with him like
There must be some safe place
to deliver him, before I . . .
before all mothers . . .
Isn't there?
Mothers do deliver. I run.

My bundle is getting too light.
Oh, the anguish on the burning stones
of carrying sheets too light
I cannot look—
I *must* unwind—
I do. Inside my sheet
is nothing.
My little boy
is vaporized.
I have to wake up,
I have to wake up!
We have to wake up.

*Mutual Assured Destruction

Barbara Mohr, *who lives in Wellesley, Massachusetts, is a mother of three, including an adopted Indian daughter she received from Mother Theresa. She works as a translator of German and is a member of the Wellesley, Massachusetts Society of Friends.*

MUNITIONS MAN

I am a practical man,
doing what I can
to live a quiet, happy life
in the suburbs with my wife.

I am a mechanical sort.
Gears and levers are my forte.
My job is in a local lab,
a government building rather drab,

designing clever widgets
for a salary in double digits
to detonate the "H," the "A,"
"quickly, efficiently," as they say.

I hope, of course, that never
will anyone pull the lever.
Nonetheless, I do my job,
designing a better knob

to explode the world with speed.
After all, I have a family to feed.

Susan Landon, *former computer specialist, is now a freelance writer. She specializes in environmental, women's and community organizing issues.*

NUCLEAR IRONY

Somewhere there is a nuclear warhead with my name on it;
Somewhere there is another one with your name.

It's a comforting thought,
Isn't it?

*A former newspaper editor and publisher, **Roy Purefoy** is a poet, novelist, and essayist who lives on a wooded tract adjoining the Brazos River near Mineral Wells, Texas.*

THE MOLE

This is not
a test. This
is the real thing. Burrow
underground. Tunnel in the soil
below contamination.
Hurry—the shrinking of hands
neither acquits
nor saves. Close
your eyes, you will acclimate
to earth
in the larynx, the defection
of words. All life is sacrosanct
and silent survival the prize
of those willing to mutate.

Deanne Bayer *is a volunteer leader of Support Group for Caregivers of the Elderly. She lives and writes in Cleveland Heights, Ohio.*

IX

Peace

THE COVENANT

"I do set my rainbow in the sky as a reminder of
my covenant with every living thing on earth."

It's time, Solomon, now
to render a new decision—
the baby has already been
sliced—more than once
and though the mother cries
and though all mothers cry
no one no longer
cares

It's time, Solomon, now
it's been 2,000 years
and the baby old as you
is confused
doesn't cry the way it should
doesn't laugh or walk straight
and its blood is a mushroom
cloud

It's time, Solomon, now
son of David, son of Bathsheba
Solomon, wisest of kings
remember the ancient covenant
of rainbows
and let the baby heal
and let the baby

live . . .

Leatrice Lifshitz *conducts her life as writer and editor in*
Pomona, New York.

SAVE PEACE

Break down the walls!
Bring out the love.
Destroy all guns!
Rejuvenate the peace.
Save your lives!
Save the universe!
Save the earth!
Save me.

Sarah Alexander attends the 11th grade at Notre Dame Academy in Toledo, Ohio. She is sixteen years old.

WHAT WILL BE THE COST

If we don't begin to think about peace,
What will be the cost?
If we don't get started on working for peace,
How much will be lost"

Merle Ray Beckwith *served as a U.S. Peace Corps Volunteer in Nigeria and now works with the Association for Retarded Citizens in Santa Barbara, California.*

FORECAST QUESTIONS

What will the year two thousand bring?
Will there be birds still left to sing?
Will we be wearing oxygen masks?
Will machines be assigned to do our tasks?
Will there be names or numbers given?
Will mercy killings be forgiven?
Will we have cars or just massive planes?
Will we fly to work in special lanes?
Will water be bottled, will we eat seaweed cakes?
Will pollution foul our food and lakes?
Will all animals be caged in a zoo?
Will all other species become extinct too?
Will Scientists be able to predict every day?
Will we be programmed in school to act the same way?
Will the people who die be buried upright?
Will computers fight wars to determine who's right?

Arleen Cohen is an activities therapist working with the
mentally ill and a professional artist, potter, and poet.

BECAUSE WE FEAR

Because we fear one another
We shall one day have
Despair for breakfast
Powder shall become
Our high towers
Poison the water
Of our rivers
Emptiness our litany
And death our atmosphere.
The sun unwrapped will peel us
Sick to death
And polar cold
Divide our elements

And where O God of Love
Are you going to stand
And where am I to hope from?

People have returned
From this land where hatred
Has its last results
They have told us
But we have not turned back
We build our towers higher
And our weapons deadlier
We sell death to the hungry
We have not learned a thing

Will you stay out there
And let us crumble into nothing
Before your judgment
Can be guessed at?
Hold me in your lowest dungeon
Lest I risk a place of honor
In this kingdom

B.E. Stock *is a secretary. She writes folk and Christian music and plays guitar and piano.*

THE WORD PEACE

The word peace has been associated among other things with passivity, un-manliness, subservience, namby pambiness, impotent idealism, cowardice, preachiness, stagnation, and considered an impediment to both creativity and competitiveness. Perhaps instead of putting our attention to "peace," we should focus on understanding the forces that drive the human animal and developing skills to recognize these forces in operation and then learn how to handle them and concentrate on "negotiation" or "arbitration" or "forcing change" or some other word that means aggressive, realistic prevention of war.

Joan Valdina is a 74 year old grandmother who is a retired teacher and researcher and lives in Needham, Massachusetts.

PEACEWORK

They call it a summit meeting,
but it is really a quilting party.
They sit around the table
carefully stitching together
little squares of peace.
Every piece a different fabric,
colors harmonizing or clashing,
endless variety of designs,
difficult to fit
into a pattern.
It is tedious work,
smoothing wrinkles,
hemming ragged edges,
trimming loose threads,
attending to details
with tiny invisible stitches,
to make a patchwork quilt
that will warm the world.

I **Elsie Bowman** Kurz lives and writes in Delray Beach, Florida.

THE ARSENAL

Words are weapons, piercing the heart.
Arrow and spear words, painfully pointed.
Bullet words enter and exit the head.
Machete words cut to the bone.
Bayonet words eviscerate.
Mortar words, lobbed over a summit,
have trajectory consequences.

Some words explode like land mines,
or hand grenades, or
bazookas hitting a tank.

Words are weapons, but no word
is atomic or radioactive,
making words, we hope,
the weapons all nations find attractive.

Elsie Feliz grew up in a Russian village in San Francisco during World War II. As a child she attended a church under two flags: the Stars and Stripes and the Hammer and Sickle.

FLOWER CHILD

Where are you, flower child?
You believed in magic.
The boundaries of peace and freedom that you crossed are
being replaced
by BMW's, IRA's, CD's, and CEO's.

Where did you go?
I don't recognize you in the busy malls or executive suites,
but I know you are there.

Can you see me, too?
Do you see the seed of peace that you planted
just below the surface of my smile
as your eyes meet mine?

My peace symbol is unbroken.

Remember when we sang and played guitars in the mountains?
God, we were strong then.

Take me home, flower child.
Let me hear the clarity of the angel's bells at dawn
as they call me to a new and glorious tomorrow.

Because I have a secret.
I will share it with you as we fly:
I have seen eternity;
I have touched the light, and it is my very soul.

Once more, my soul greets the newborn day.
Once more, the awakening.
The gentle angelus goes forth, riding the wings of the dawn.

The wind pulls at my hair and laughs into my eyes
making mockery of my all-important mortal breath.
Carry me, carry me home.

I reaffirm the ageless promise.
I accept the sands of soul memory that reside, lonesome in
my pockets,
left from the morning we collected shells from the beach.

Flower child, do you remember?

Awakening, blurry-eyed, muddled and befuddled, I stand in
the world of today.
The needle strings the tiny pearls that make up a new
morning.

Clarity comes on silent wings.
Can peace be far behind?

Tara Allan *has worked as a technical writer, an editor, and a freelance writer. She has used American Sign Language while working with deaf children and adults.*

BLESSED ARE THE PEACEMAKERS

Rebels of the Sixties
shouted, "Let's make love not war!"
The Seventies spurred radicals
who politically sparred.
The Eighties brought about
another type of youth:
more thoughtful, less acerbic,
and surely less uncouth.
Can this new breed now lead us
with a Nineties' quiet stand,
making peace-love passivistic
and pacifists in command?

Shirley Vogler Meisten writes, cares for elderly mothers, and
lives in Indianapolis. She has been a peace activist all her life.

LISTEN LEADERS

Don't tell us
that an umbrella
even a large one
will protect us from the rain
when the rain is acid
and burns holes in the toughest fabric
and don't tell us
this superumbrella
deflects rockets
as if they were mere ping pong balls
bouncing off some swift racket.
Rather, pray tell us
you'll stop playing power games
involving us
making winners
but losers too
on this tight rope around the world
where the weight of one umbrella is enough
to tip all of us into the deep void forever.

Liliane Richman teaches *Creative Writing and Advanced French at the Dallas High School for the Performing Arts.*

THE SILENT HEART

Must there always be a war as in all the years before
Would it be so strange to simply live in peace
We just never seem to be content with harmony
We're consumed with need for strife to never cease
So, we claim to have good sense, ever building for defense
To the point where we can end life in a wink
And with the arrogance of man we do everything we can
To endanger life, as if we cannot think
No one forces us to be in this state of apathy
We accept these things with our eyes wide open
While the few who think and care warn us to beware
And with saddened hearts keep pleading and keep hoping
But it's up to you and me to open our hearts and see
Before the time for change has passed us by
For if we refuse to learn, if the tide will not be turned
Then all that's good and beautiful will die
And all the joys of worth on our lovely planet Earth
Will then be just a sad dream unfulfilled
And the people will have missed the chance to live in bliss
Leaving in its place a world whose heart is stilled

Rhoda-Katie Hannan, retired secretary, writes hymns and
songs, words and music. One hymn, "The Sound of Peace," has
been performed by the Unitarian and Episcopal Choirs, included
in a United Nations publication, and may be performed by the
Mormon Tabernacle Choir.

AND THE MEEK

Let all those who favor war
Without exception or seniority
Be the first to go into battle
Against mutual consenting enemies
Let all those that oppose war
Live in peace with mutual friends
And those who are undecided
Remain to inherit the Earth.

Ignatius Graffeo is a commercial artist and runs a small press, "The Poet Tree." He is a member of the Shelley Society and lives in Queens, New York.

PAPER CRANES
(for Anthony)

Paper cranes
yellow, red
orange origami
child-made cranes
strung like trawls of fish
in Nagasaki and Hiroshima

some fall off and
drift like autumn leaves
shrouding the countryside
like flames weeping
tumbling like autumn leaves

some fall off and
drop like tears
mourning the charred earth
like wailing widows
raining like silver tears

some fall off and
whisk away in the wind
speckling the dazed sun
like ashen memories
howling in the fiery wind

some fall off and
glide gracefully to the ground
thin, delicate
paper cranes
like snowflakes
falling to the ground

some fall off and
spread like cherry blossoms
pinken the brown earth
like gossamer on the horizon]
papering the world with cherry blossoms

some fall off and
sail up to the sky
rising on blue wings
like dandelion dreams
floating up to the sky

some fall off and
make it back to America
scattering over the cities
like confetti
like multi-colored messages

paper peace cranes
swarming over America

Mike Maggio works in international education at the
International Airports Projects in Jeddah, Saudi Arabia. He has
lived in the Middle East for five years.

ARE WE UPSET OR ARE WE ANGRY?

Crossword puzzles never risk their lives
to prove stereotypic utterances
but humans do

That musician playing the cello fascinates me
his body smiles then bends then cries

Some people can take wood, wire and glue
and make cellos for a living

Others take steel, wire and bolts
and make guns

At what point will the black attaché case empty itself
of the ticking bomb?
And why do our fearless leaders insist on its presence
at every gathering?

Silly, isn't it, yet staggering too
how each mouth shapes a word
how each hand shapes the air
how each moves beyond sound, beyond sight

Sometimes journeys take a while
maybe a war or two

Behind any moral judgment cowers blind faith
that your neighbor's dog will kill every intruder
except you

And then we must decide
Are we upset or are we angry?

No matter what we answer
someone's beliefs will be served
for dinner

Yet I for one shall levitate my knife and fork
I for one shall sing off-key
secretly praying
that all the guests find me
amazingly distracting.

Rebecca Dosch is an American currently teaching English in a Japanese high school and studying the Japanese language.

DREAMS

I.

In cool woods white trilliums flower,
pure flame and dew,
to diaphanous hands. Dreams
ride stirring winds

>   (over walls
>   torn by war).

In the cool earth
lies a cache (near the crumbled walls):
teacups like petalled flowers . . .

>   (Discard the newspapers,
>   wrappings of disaster!)

Green, pink, or blue, survivors
bud with painted clouds
strewn with sun's gold, old dreams:

>   love and ceremony . . .

Real clouds billow,
swell my dark fears, the fierce light—

>   bitter ecstasy

>   (hope beyond war . . .)

II.

In cool woods
pools flower, reflecting
clouds,
>   gowns
of ghost-women: diaphanous hands

---

tremble, remembering
the weight of children,
the touch of their hands,
        loves and burdens

                beyond war . . .

Birds sing of old news.
The world's children

                recall
hands that offered cups
green, pink, or blue:
            blooming,
                even now . . .

Past the ruined walls
newspapers, changed by light,
tumble with faces, love, words

                sown by wind:

    Make your new world

            beyond war
            beyond war.

Susan Verelon Stark *enjoys hiking, backpacking, canoeing and cross-country skiing in Penfield, New York.*

PEACE WITNESS

Lady Liberty stepped off her island
last week, joined the human race, searching,
seeking life. She led a peaceful
gentle people, every race and
color, on dharma, the right way.

Having explored the paths of devotion
and truth, she turned them onto the
path of action with a glad-faced clown
whose touch marked crimson circles of
rebirth and wisdom.
                              Hearts and bodies
quickened to dance, a long chorus line
moving in a rite of creation.

Jane McDonnell (Sisters of Charity) *does historical research and writing for the BVM Archives in Dubuque, Iowa. She has been involved with the peace movement since the 1950s.*

B-52

I carpeted the battlefields with grass and dropped
money on civilians. They bought food, and flowers.

I poured water on drought-stricken farms and burning
trees,
dropped seeds into furrows, and the dry stalks bloomed.

I brought bandages to bleeding inner cities.
Mothers burned stockpiles of drugs and jumped for joy.

I dropped books beside freeways and people stopped to
read.
I strafed shopping malls, and they turned into schools.

I bombed prisons, and when I set the inmates free
they kissed the guards and started day care centers.

I flew 4000 sorties over Amazon rain forests.
When the cutting stopped, banana leaves rejoiced.

Elephants trumpeted a new world order,
and whales proclaimed the freedom of the seas.

Laurie Robertson-Lorant teaches English and coaches tennis at St. Mark's School in Southborough, Massachusetts.

PEACE BEGINS WITH ME

A world divided in itself
Shall never know the peace
That all men dream of in their hearts;
The hope that wars will cease.

Full peace will come to all the world
When hearts are hatred-free;
But peace must start in one man's heart;
Let peace begin with me!

Delphine LeDoux, retired employee of the State of California, member of the National Association of Parliamentarians, has nine children, eleven grandchildren, and lives in Sacramento with her spouse of 50 years.

MAKE WAR A GAME

Did you watch it on television?
Were you glued to the screen?
Did you wonder, at times,
what does it mean?
The perfect hits!
What besides buildings
were blown into bits?
We had a war
and lots of people came
Didn't you think what
a great video game?
While the rivers of fire
ruined the ecology
who could help but admire
the super technology?

Let's record it—or board it
Let's make it a game with
"Modern War" as its name
Sell it and play it
with levers and lights
Who could nay say it,
these quite harmless fights
Make it a game that we play
And no one will die from such shoots
But you, wizards of war, find a way
a more humane, grown-up way
to settle disputes.

Marguerite M. Striar is an artist, teacher, editor and writer in Washington, D.C.

THE ROOTS OF PEACE

Peace is more than an end to war
Its roots spread wide and far
Burrowing deep into the earth
In search of nourishment;
Each tiny whorl, alive but dry,
Aching for relief

Thirsting for global sanity
Which scales time-honored walls
Crying out for every soul
To be nurtured and set free
And every poor one to be fed
And looked on as a friend

Peace longs for laughing children who
Have skills to be themselves
Who recognize the innate gifts
That build sound harmony
So never again will blood be spilled
For the name we give our faith

The status quo cannot suffice
Each branching shoot must grow
Thrusting downward through the soil
Of prejudice and hate
Seeking a purer sustenance
Than color, creed or race:

The oneness of mankind

Barbara Bostian *is the Managing Editor for the Human Resource Institute at Eckerd College in St. Petersburg, Florida.*

BREAD AND KISSES

Why not pledge allegiance to the world,
nationalism as out-of-date
as another millennium's city-states,

although we post-industrial elite
keep on skimming bread and meat
from third-world hunger.

Let's join the human race
by sharing loaves and fishes,
not bribes or homicidal kisses.

Alan Atkinson has lectured at Rutgers University, the University of Maryland, and the National University of Ireland.

A REASONABLE REQUEST

Could we live?!
I mean, could you see your way
To lettin' us see
Another day?
We know, you wanna kill,
Blow up every goddamn thing in sight,
But Jesus, people have hopes,
And my daughter has a baby son.
Could he live?!
Live long enough
To be hers, be mine,
Be himself,
Let his eyes shine,
His heart drink its fill?
And if we have our way with him,
He won't wanna kill.
He'll live and he'll let live.
And what's more,
We could teach a whole new generation of guys
And soldier-girls, who wanna be guys,
To give, and not give a hoot about guns.
So come on, don't kill us.
It's not that hard.
All you gotta do
Is make your hand soft,
So soft it can't even pull a trigger.
And it won't mean you're weak,
'Cause your eyes'll be soft, too.
Soft eyes are strong,
Strong.
Soft eyes let you live,
Let us all live,
Forever!

Joanna Nealon is a blind woman who studied in Paris, France on a Fulbright Scholarship many years ago. Now she recites her poetry in the Boston, Massachusetts area, "attempting the mad leap from bureau-cleaner to literary outer-space."

THE FIRST OF MAY

We're holding a Kite-day
because it's Spring—
mothers and fathers and children
with paper   string   paint   paste.

If it rains
we're meeting inside
to go on with the kite making.

If it nukes
we're meeting inside too.

They don't know any better
than to build the bombs.

We don't know any better
than to paint flowers on kites
and send them up in the sky.

Mary Neville tutors in an inner-city school in Cleveland, Ohio. She works with third graders, teaching creative writing and exchanging poetry with suburban children.

HYMN TO PEACE

Translated from the original "Paean to Peace," by the Greek
poet Bakchylides (fl. 5th century B.C.)

Peace brings great gifts to mortals:
Wealth—and song flowering from honeyed tongues;
Yes, and on altars of wondrous working
She brings to the gods themselves
Golden flaming thighbones to be burned,
Thighbones of oxen and of shaggy sheep;
To youths she brings
Darts of sharp desire
For games and flutes and merrymaking.

Deep-growing on the iron-bound shield
Lie thickened webs spun by dark Arachne;
Mold conquers the two-edged sword,
Subdues the lethal spear.
Clash of bronzed trumpets is not heard;
Hearts are warmed and gladdened.
The god of sleep, sweet to the mind,
Does not dance past our eyelids.
Streets are filled with loving revelers,
And chants in childish voices
Burst up in flame to light the firmament.

Jeanne Carney holds a doctorate in English Literature and
Linguistics—"A surprising statement, perhaps, from a hill-
farmer's daughter who 'turned bookish,' as my plain-speaking
mother put it."

A LESSON TO WARRIORS TO PAY HEED
TO HUMAN OCCUPATION

There are Gothic cathedrals in me
that fling slender vaults to heaven,
spires pointing to God.

Inside me are markers by which you
found my town across medieval fields.

This coming to the point.
The wanderer coming to his place.

You left Cologne Cathedral standing
to orient yourselves and bombed the rest.

But did you know that winding high
to the bells my stairs are worn by those
climbing to our God?

*Ursula Irwin, raised in Cologne, Germany, straddles two
cultures, "sometimes more and sometimes less successfully."
She teaches in Portland, Oregon.*

Peace

THE MAN UNDERGROUND

The world will be saved by beauty. Fyodor Dostoyevsky

In the end
it will not be
what you have done
but staring at
the jade tree that will
keep you sane.

In the end
the man underground Missouri
or New Mexico
will not turn that key
because some memory
of his child
crashing through
piles of dry leaves
will not let him.

In the end
those impatiens
you planted in May,
that hummingbird
above your head,
this cool autumn breeze
will save us.

Diane E. Imhoff, with her husband, has devoted her life to a very active assault on war and the military. They live with two small sons in Chico, California.

PEACE SEEDS

Peace Seeds represent the twelve prayers for peace prayed in Asisi, Italy on the Day of Prayer for World Peace during the United Nations International Year of Peace, 1986. The prayers were brought to the United States and entrusted to the care of disabled and terminally-ill children at The Life Experience School. The distribution of Peace Seeds is a world service project under the care and direction of the Franciscan Quaker Fellowship. The prayers belong to humanity ... duplication is encouraged.

"Like the bee gathering honey from the different flowers, the wise person accepts the essence of the different scriptures and sees only the good in all religions." Mahatma Gandhi

1. The Hindu Prayer for Peace
Oh God, lead us from the unreal to the Real. Oh God, lead us from darkness to light. Oh God, lead us from death to immortality. Shanti, Shanti, Shanti unto all. Oh Lord God almighty, may there be peace in celestial regions. May there be peace on earth. May the waters be appeasing. May herbs be wholesome, and may trees and plants bring peace to all. May all beneficent beings bring peace to us. May thy Vedic Law propagate peace all through the world. May all things be a source of peace to us. And may thy peace itself, bestow peace on all, and may that peace come to me also.

2. The Buddhist Prayer for Peace
May all beings everywhere plagued with sufferings of body and mind quickly be freed from their illnesses. May those frightened cease to be afraid, and may those bound be free. May the powerless find power, and may people think of befriending one another. May those who find themselves in trackless, fearful wildernesses - the children, the aged, the unprotected - be guarded by beneficent celestials, and may they swiftly attain Buddhahood.

3. The Jainist Prayer for Peace

Peace and Universal Love is the essence of the Gospecl preached by all the Enlightened Ones. The Lord has preached that equanimity is the Dharma. Forgive do I creatures all, and let all creatures forgive me. Unto all have I amity, and unto none enmity. Know that violence is the root cause of all miseries in the world. Violence, in fact, is the knot of bondage. "Do not injure any living being." This is the eternal, perennial, and unalterable way of spiritual life. A weapon howsoever powerful it may be, can always be superseded by a superior one; but no weapon can, however, be superior to non violence and love.

4. The Muslim Prayer for Peace

In the name of Allah, the beneficent, the merciful. Praise be to the Lord of the Universe who has created us and made us into tribes and nations, that we may know each other, not that we may despise each other. If the enemy incline towards peace, do thou also incline towards peace, and trust in God, for the Lord is the one that heareth and knoweth all things and the servents of God, Most Gracious are those who walk on the Earth in humility, and when we address them, we say "PEACE."

5. The Sikh Prayer for Peace

"God adjudges us according to our deeds, not the coat that we wear: that Truth is above everything, but higher still is truthful living. "Know that we attaineth God when we loveth, and only that victory endures in consequence of which no one is defeated."

6. The Bahai' Prayer for Peace

Be generous in prosperity, and thankful in adversity. Be fair in thy judgement, and guarded in thy speech. Be a lamp unto those who walk in darkness, and a home to the stranger. Be eyes to the blind, and a guiding light unto the feet of the erring. Be a breath of life to the body of human-kind, a dew to the soil of the human heart, and a fruit upon the tree of humility.

7. The Shinto Prayer for Peace

"Although the people living across the ocean surrounding us, I believe, are all our brothers and sisters, why are there constant troubles in this world? Why do winds and waves rise in the ocean surrounding us? I only earnestly wish that the wind will soon puff away all the clouds which are hanging over the tops of the mountains."

8. The Native African Prayer for Peace

Almighty God, the Great Thumb we cannot evade to tie any knot; the Roaring Thunder that splits mighty trees; the all seeing Lord up on high who sees even the footprints of an antelope on a rockmass here on Earth. You are the one who does not hesitate to respond to our call. You are the cornerstone of peace.

9. The Native American Prayer for Peace

O Great Spirit of our Ancestors, I raise my pipe to you. To your messengers the four winds, and to Mother Earth who provides for your children. Give us the wisdom to teach our children to love, to respect, and to be kind to each other so that they may grow with peace in mind. Let us learn to share all the good things that you provide for us on this Earth.

10. The Zoroastrian Prayer for Peace

We pray to God to eradicate all the misery in the world: that understanding triumph over ignorance, that generosity triumph over indifference, that trust triumph over contempt, and that truth triumph over falsehood.

11. The Jewish Prayer for Peace

Come let us go up to the mountain of the Lord, that we may walk the paths of the Most High. And we shall beat our swords into ploughshares, and our spears into pruning hooks. nation shall not lift up sword against nation - neither shall they learn war any more. And none shall be afraid, for the mouth of the Lord of Hosts has spoken.

12. The Christian Prayer for Peace

"Blessed are the peacemakers, for they shall be known as the Children of God. But I say to you that hear, love your enemies, do good to those who hate you, bless those who curse you, pray for those who abuse you. To those who strike you on the cheek, offer the other also, and from those who take away your cloak, do not withhold your coat as well. Give to everyone who begs from you, and of those who take away your goods, do not ask them again. And as you wish that others would do to you, do so to them."

EPILOGUE: FROM WARPOWER TO PEACEPOWER

Suppose policy makers really hear the dread of war and love of peace expressed by contributors to this book and people everywhere.

Suppose citizens change from war consciousness to peace consciousness and from warpower to peacepower by peacework, even a small piece at a time.

Suppose, rather than teaching history as a series of prewar, war and postwar eras, schools teach history as a series of peace eras disrupted by destructive wars. Suppose books celebrate peace presidents and other peacemakers instead of war presidents and generals, emphasizing war casualties instead of victories. Suppose our elders speak at schools about the horrors of wars witnessed in their lifetimes.

Suppose instead of media announcing birthdays of famous people or centenarians, they announce peacebirths, the number of warless days and hopefully years—decades. Suppose each day without war, a tree or bush is planted in a National Peace Forest. Suppose children are taken to this Peace Forest instead of to famous battlegrounds or war monuments. Suppose instead of collecting war mementos, collectors take acorns or other seeds or saplings from peace forests to start peace parks everywhere.

Suppose Fourth of July parades with military units and equipment become instead Peaceparades honoring Peace Corps and other volunteers for humanity. Suppose these parades feature children wearing clothes of all nations carrying flags of all nations to celebrate world interdependence and independence from hate.

Suppose we have a contest for a new national anthem that celebrates peace, not war. Suppose children's summer camps stop competitions and color wars and play cooperative games. Suppose parents send children to peace schools instead of military academies. Suppose R.O.T.C. (Reserve Officer Training Corps) means some day Reaching Out To Care (instead of to kill).

Suppose we replace video and board games that obliterate enemies and objects with games that eliminate racism, disease, poverty, drought, homelessness and other social and natural disasters. Suppose winning such games means planting an acre of rain forest, curing AIDS or cancer, feeding the hungry, housing the homeless.

Suppose instead of continually teaching and rewarding for conflict in school debates and with grading curves, we teach resolution and cooperation in schools and colleges, making Consensus 101 or Peacemaking 101 required courses.

Suppose mainstream card manufacturers sell cards with peace heroes and heroines and we exchange these on Earth Day and holidays. Suppose, instead of peace leader calendars being sold only to the already convinced by peace organizations, peace calendars are substituted for landscape ones now given out by companies to their clients.

Suppose films with violence and war made exciting are no longer produced or are X-rated and movies are made showing cooperation and endeavors toward peace.

Suppose you make your own list, share it with others, and act on it whenever and wherever you can. Suppose we abandon apathy and escapism and vow we will no longer support war because it is barbaric, futile and obsolete.

Suppose people are intelligent, alert and compassionate enough to make peacemaking a priority and begin serious peacework NOW. Then, perhaps, as Eve Merriam says (on page 247) someday a child will ask, "Mother, what was war?"

Ruth Harriet Jacobs

Index

316
308
263

246

130
135
170